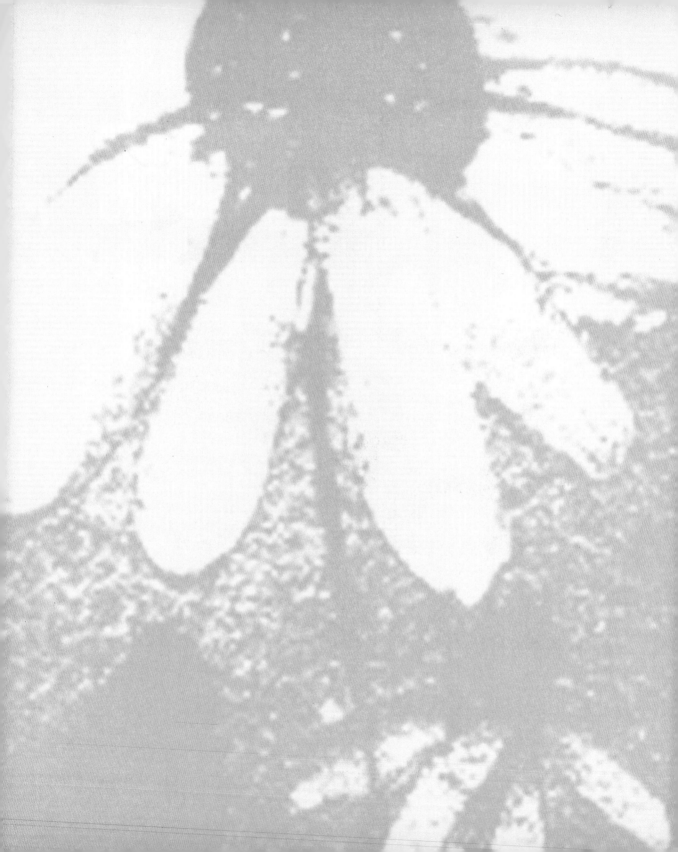

chillout

100 creative ways to relax

Richard Craze

SOURCEBOOKS, INC.®
NAPERVILLE, ILLINOIS

Copyright © 2001 MQ
Publications Ltd
Text copyright © 2001
Richard Craze

Editor: Nicola Birtwisle
Designer: Justina Leitão
Concept: Mark Buckingham
Illustrator: Jane Hadfield

Published by Sourcebooks, Inc.
P.O. Box 4410, Naperville,
Illinois 60567–4410
(630) 961–3900
FAX: (630) 961–2168

ISBN: 1–57071–673–0

Printed and bound in UK
MQ 10 9 8 7 6 5 4 3 2 1

With thanks to Rita Ho

Contents

Introduction

Welcome to a unique guide to relaxation—*Chill Out*. In this book you will find a remarkable variety of creative ways to switch off, chill out, and kick back. Some you may have heard of, such as meditation and creative visualization, but you will also find many that you may not previously have associated with relaxation such as kite flying, herb growing, and papier mâché.

The more we assimilate brain activity—right brain and left brain—the more relaxed we become. *Chill Out*'s techniques encourage us to use our left

 brain, which controls our creative side, and relax our right brain, which deals with logic and reasoning. But it is a combination of the two that *really* enhances our well-being.

The activities in this book will certainly get you in the mood for creative relaxation. All you need is an open mind, a spirit of adventure, and a desire to be truly relaxed and chilled. These experiences are here for you to dip into. You don't have to work your way straight through the book. Nor do you have to do them all. If you like them and they work for you,

then keep doing them. If they don't work for you, then try something different. There are no hard and fast rules. There is no pressure, no time limit, and no one looking over your shoulder and checking the results. The experiences in this book are for you to take pleasure from, to relax, to enjoy—to chill out.

Some are for the more active, such as dancing, planting a tree, jogging, and urban exploration, but there is also plenty

for the less active person, such as writing a love poem, exploring family trees, appreciating music, and flower arranging. Try whatever you fancy. You may find new interests, things that will keep you involved and amused, things to fire your imagination and stimulate you, things to entertain and relax you.

Happy chilling!

Keep a dream journal

All day long we keep it together. We may feel anxious and pressured, but we don't let it show. We have become distanced from nature, cut off from our own senses. We are conditioned to the stress of the modern world, and we try not to let it affect us. You owe it to yourself, your health, and those around you to learn to relax.

An easy way to see what is really worrying us is to monitor our dreams. The only place we can really relax and be ourselves is in our dreams. That is why keeping a dream journal is so important—it gives us a window into our subconscious.

All you need to start a dream journal is to keep a pad of paper and a pen by your bed. Every morning, when you wake up, jot down whatever you have been dreaming about. If you think you didn't dream, then just write whatever thought first comes into your head. This may be an echo of your last dream—a sort of dream vapor trail—but it may be enough to trigger memories of the other dreams you had.

Keep the journal for at least a month before you start trying to make sense of your dreams. When you look back over them, you may begin to see recurring themes. Perhaps a vision of being chased, of falling from a high place, of being confined in a small place, or even of being in an unpleasant incident in public. Or it might be a recurring symbol—a flower, a boat, or an animal.

Once you can see a pattern—and a pattern nearly always exists—you are halfway to interpreting the dreams. There are many schools of thought as to what the symbolic dream representations actually mean, but an easy way to make sense of your dreams is to remember that everything and everyone in your dreams is yourself. If you dream that you are being chased by a bear—you are the person being chased and you are also the bear. If you dream that you are alone in a derelict building—you are both the person and the derelict building. In the first example, you might ask yourself why you feel you are a bear and why you are chasing yourself. In the second example, you might like to ask yourself why you feel alone and what it is about you that you feel is derelict. Once you try this unusual, but highly effective, way of interpreting your dreams, a lot of sense and truth is revealed. Then you can take positive steps to deal effectively with the underlying problems.

Once you are proficient at keeping a dream journal—and interpreting your dreams—then you could start waking yourself up during sleep to quickly write down your dreams—and then go back to sleep, of course.

The best time for recording your dreams is about two to four hours after you have first fallen asleep. Perhaps you could set an alarm clock to wake you. And don't worry, you will fall asleep again very quickly and suffer no ill effects. Happy dreaming.

Try aromatherapy

Aromatherapy is a very old therapy. The ancient Egyptians practiced it. They buried jars of myrrh and frankincense with the Pharaohs in their tombs and used the same perfumes cosmetically and medically.

Today aromatherapy is widespread and there are many practitioners of this ancient art. The essential oils are highly concentrated and extracted from plants. The oils are absorbed by the skin as massage oil or vaporized to be breathed in. You can also add a few drops of oil to your bath. Aromatherapy works because the plants it is based on have therapeutic qualities.

HOW TO USE THE OILS

If you want to add a few drops of oil to your bath, put them in after the bath has stopped running and before you get in. If you put them in too early they will evaporate. Try camomile for relaxation, frankincense for rejuvenation, grapefruit for refreshing stimulation, lavender for a good night's sleep, neroli as an antidepressant, peppermint to relieve tiredness, and sandalwood for relaxation and as a sedative.

To vaporize the oils you need to buy a burner. The top of the burner is filled with water to which you add a few drops of oil. Light a nightlight or small candle under the burner and the resulting heat vaporizes the oil. This pleasant and perfumed air fills the room and lasts a long time. Try using basil to aid concentration, bergamot to relax and inspire you, cinnamon as a stimulant, eucalyptus to ease congestion and relieve cold symptoms, geranium to stabilize you, and rosewood to soothe you.

You also can massage the oils into your skin. Add a few drops to a carrier oil such as almond, jojoba, or avocado. Try clary sage for relieving the symptoms of premenstrual syndrome, cypress for poor circulation, juniperberry for muscular pain, arthritis, and rheumatism, lemongrass as a stimulant, lime as a tonic, marjoram to revitalize tired muscles, and orange for digestive disorders.

You can sprinkle a few drops onto your pillow or bedclothes to help you sleep, and the aroma is released slowly throughout the night. Try lavender for a really good night's sleep, rosemary to refresh you and help relax tired muscles, rosewood for relaxation, and tea tree for sweet dreams.

SOME GUIDELINES

Aromatherapy oils are very concentrated, but they are safe as long as you stick to a few basic guidelines. They should never be taken internally. Nor should oils be used by pregnant women without professional advice. They should not be used on children except in very diluted amounts. Never use the oils directly on your skin in an undiluted form and stop using any that cause allergic reactions. Store in a cool, dark place. If you are in doubt about any aspect of aromatherapy oils, check with a qualified aromatherapist.

Draw with sand

Sand art is an ancient shaman's art. It is a ritualistic and highly symbolic way of drawing pictures—not in sand but with sand—to put you in touch with the spirit world and with your inner self. There is an ancient Tibetan tradition of creating intricate mandalas with colored sands. The "sand paintings" are destroyed almost as soon as they are made, a process that represents the transience of existence and the Buddhist cycle of life.

You, however, don't have to aim for intricate detail. Drawing pictures with sand requires very little skill except an intuitive understanding of form and movement in the natural world. All you have to do is switch off your conscious mind and allow the sand to fall from your hand into whatever shapes and forms it chooses to take. This may be spirals, abstract shapes, birds, animals, even demons and gods.

WHAT YOU NEED

First, you will need some colored sand. If you want the natural look, gather sand fresh from the beach. Follow the coast-line and see how the sand changes color even within a few miles. You don't need very much sand, but a variety of colors is essential. If you don't live near a beach, you can buy colored sand from good craft stores.

Once you've collected the sand, you need to mark out an area in your back yard where you can draw your pictures. Keep the sand in different containers so you can help yourself to a handful when you feel the need to change color. Remember that it's not you drawing the picture—the sand is drawing. Let the sand fall lightly from your fingertips as you swirl it and make sure your move-ments are natural and instinctive. When you've finished stand back and let the picture speak to you.

Dance for joy

Dancing is a great way to relieve stress. It is therapeutic and relaxing. And you need no training—just your instincts and intuitive knowledge of rhythm and movement. Ritual dancing is a form of moving meditation. Close your eyes and allow your body to express itself in movement and form. Listen to what your body wants to do.

WHEN TO DANCE

You can dance whenever the mood takes you. On waking each morning it is an excellent way to limber up, get fit, and start the day. Begin with a salutation to the sun. Stand with your hands by your sides. Bring your arms up above your head and then spread them wide to represent the sun's rays. Place one leg backwards and bend the other knee as if bowing. Bring your arms down and out in front of you. Bring your hands together as if in prayer. Push your arms upwards again and stand upright, and repeat the entire movement.

As you start to feel comfortable moving in ritual dance, add movements, improvise, feel your body becoming more fluid. Dance ritually to celebrate the joy of being alive.

Study the stars

On a clear night when we look up at the stars it's not unusual to feel tiny and insignificant—the sheer number of stars is awesome. But once we understand how stars are born, why the constellations have the names they do, and how the universe is evolving, we feel reassured and more secure.

We know the earth is turning and that the sky changes above us as it revolves. The stars appear not to move because they are so far away—the closest is more than twenty-four million miles away. If we stay still long enough during an evening watching the stars, we will see the steady progression of the night sky.

Generations upon countless generations of humans have stood and looked up and wondered in awe. We feel more relaxed knowing we are part of a great cycle, feel our place within the universe, and even begin to understand the myths of our ancestors.

As you gaze upwards, bear in mind that over 6,000 years ago in ancient

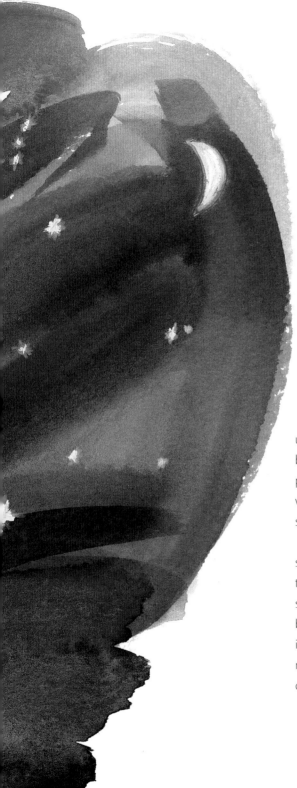

Egypt, others stood and watched the night sky. These ancient Egyptians plotted the positions of all the major constellations.

Watching the night sky not only fills us with wonder and awe at the stars but at the universe with its immense distances and limitless possibilities, its infiniteness, its origins and expansions—and we are filled with questions and prayers about the Creator of this magnificent, awe-inspiring design.

Watching the night sky also makes us wonder about how we are influenced by the passage of the stars and other planets. We all feel the pull of the moon when it is full and feel joyful when the sun warms us.

Finding your way around the stars is simple. There are only a few hundred that are bright enough to form the constellations. Once you know them, you'll be able to identify them easily. And gazing up at them on a clear night will soon make you realize how insignificant your own stresses and problems really are.

Make a miniature Zen garden

A Japanese Zen garden is the perfect expression of tranquillity, natural order, peace, calm, and unchanging serenity. In a Zen garden you can meditate, think, enjoy solitude, kick back, and just be. We might not be able to sit in a miniature garden, but it can sit on our desk and represent all that relaxation we owe ourselves—a sort of living reminder of where we ought to be.

BASIC FORMAT

The concept of the Japanese garden is based on the Japanese saying that a sacred space is complete only when there is nothing more you can take away from it. Perfect minimization. The Japanese garden was originally created by Zen monks as a place of simple contemplation, a place where the balance of nature and the triumph of order over chaos is emphasized. The aim of a Japanese garden is to create a perfect harmony of the male and female essences within nature—a balance of yin and yang. There has to be water (yin/female) together with land (yang/male). In a dry garden, raked gravel represents the water, and rocks represent the land as islands or mountains. The gravel is raked to simulate waves or ripples lapping around the island rocks.

WHAT YOU NEED

You will need a shallow container, some gravel, a small rake, and a few interestingly shaped rocks or stones. These stones need to be chosen with great care—one should be taller than the others and very well shaped. Choose well-worn stones with no jagged edges—stones that have been weathered gently by the forces of nature.

Your gravel should be uniform, clean, an attractive color (such as pink rather than bland gray), and free of any extraneous grit or foreign bodies. Try to find gravel that has very small pieces, as we are creating this garden in miniature.

PUTTING IT TOGETHER

Place the gravel in the container and roughly flatten. Position your stones in a pleasing arrangement. They don't all have to stand upright—one could be lying down. This is known traditionally as an ox stone. If you listen to the stones they will tell you where they want to be. Try placing one upright and another next to it lying down, or one at each end of the container in a sort of mirror image. Keep adding stones until your garden looks complete and balanced.

According to the Zen monks each stone has six faces, and the one to present to the visitor is its friendly one. Turn the stones around until you see this face. Once the stones have been placed, you can begin to rake the gravel. Each stone should have gravel raked around it in a series of circular

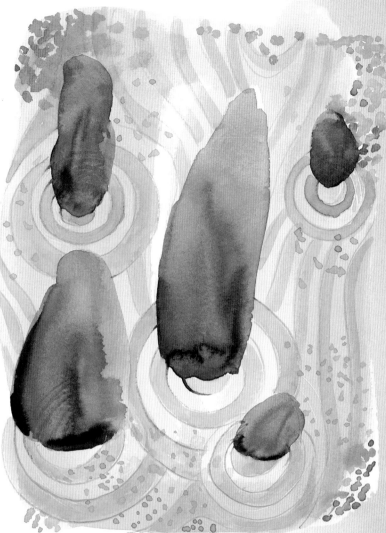

movements to represent the waves flowing around the rock. Now whenever you look at your garden you will be reminded of tranquillity, and it is very soothing and relaxing to rake the gravel into new swirling patterns.

19

Make your own paper

Creating something beautiful and unique is always relaxing. And when you make your own recycled paper, you can rest assured that you are helping to save the planet as well! Here's how.

WHAT YOU NEED

About two newspapers' worth of scrap paper

A food processor or blender

Two tablespoons of white glue

Three cups of water

A sink with four inches of cold water in it

Some old panty hose

Wire coat hangers (one for each sheet of paper)

An electric iron

Food coloring

Before you start creating, you need to make some frames. Bend the coat hangers into a square shape with a hook on one end. The squares should measure about six inches along each side. Cover the frames with the panty hose. Insert the frame into a leg to get a double thickness. Stretch it tight. Tie knots in the panty hose and use a new leg for each new frame.

Now put a handful of scrap paper and some water into the food processor. Close the lid and turn it on for a moment. Turn it off, and then add more paper and a little more water. Keep doing this until you have a gray pulp. Once the paper is no longer recognizable as paper, leave the processor on maximum for another two minutes.

Add the glue to the water in the sink, and tip out the pulp from the processor into it. Mix it up well with your hands to squish it. You should now have a runny gray mess. Add food coloring if you want colored paper.

Sink the frame to the bottom of the sink and lift it up with a thin film of paper in it. Lift very slowly, for a count of twenty. Let the water drain away for about a minute. Keep lowering and lifting frames until you have as many sheets of paper as you want to make.

Hang out the frames on a clothesline in the sun to dry. When the paper is completely dry and not damp to touch, gently peel each sheet off. And there you have it: your own paper!

Bathe by candlelight

We all need to be soothed and stroked, nurtured and purified. We need water and we need natural light. We need to relax and have our cares float away.

STEPPING BACK IN TIME

If we take a bath by electric light we are still living in the modern world. But the second we turn off the electric lights and light a candle or two, we have taken a step back in time. We have become a creature of the universe once more. We can float in the warmth and the flickering light and be at one with the cosmos, at peace with ourselves, and feel that all is well with the world.

Try adding a few drops of aromatherapy oil (see pages 12–13) to your bath water and breathe in deeply as its therapeutic and relaxing powers are released into your perfect sanctuary. Wallow in the heady perfumes as they are drawn deeply into your psyche and allowed to work their magic on you on a very deep, intuitive level.

This isn't about bathing or hygiene—this is about decadence and indulgence, a return to a simpler, more organic way of life. This is about treating you, body and soul, mind and emotions. Bathing in the soft light of candles is a treat we should all enjoy as often as we can.

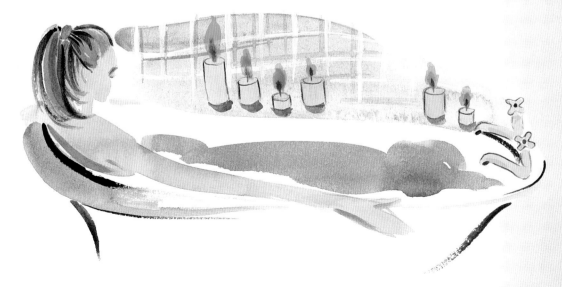

Make a den

When life gets to be too much, we need to retreat, to hide away, to find peace and solitude. This stems from a natural and understandable need to protect ourselves. If we don't, we can't find a space in which to repair, to heal, to recover, and we will be lessened for it. Creating a den is an ideal way of making a private space to retreat to.

Children acknowledge the need to create this private space by throwing blankets over a table and crawling inside. This den then becomes a pirate camp, a fort, a playhouse, a bear's cave, a tunnel, an underground river, a safe haven, a hiding place from parents and siblings, a Bedouin tent, a dragon's lair—anything the imagination can stretch to.

We lose the ability to play as we grow older, but the need to play house or build a den is perhaps the last vestige of play to leave us. We all like to create a warm, inviting living space for our family and ourselves—somewhere that reflects our personality. Making a den is taking this a stage further—creating a private personal space just for you.

WHERE'S BEST FOR A DEN?

Where dens are concerned, there is no best. It's all about personal preference, cost, space availability, and need. There's not a lot of point in a huge den if you live in a one-room flat—the flat already *is* your den. But if you have a lot of space or live in the countryside, you have a vast wealth of sites and types of den to choose from.

TYPES OF DENS

Dens come in all shapes and sizes, from humble garden sheds to grand summer-houses; from wacky gipsy caravans to stylish treehouses; from New Age yurts to old age shacks. You can create your sacred personal space in pretty much anything—I've even seen an old railway carriage used as a private hideaway. What *is* important is what you do with the inside.

WHAT WILL YOU DO WITH YOUR DEN?

You need to decide what you are going to use this space for. If you have great plans for a hobby room where you can make things and run a couple of power tools on a workbench, then maybe you need to convert a cellar. But if you want to sit and dream and watch the river meander by, perhaps a treehouse will do. How about power? Do you need light or can you make do with an oil lamp? Do you need it to run your laptop or can you manage without?

In general, the simpler your den is, the happier you'll be with it. A garden shed with a few cushions scattered on the floor and a comfortable armchair may be all you need. Paint the walls, add an exotic carpet, and you can create a wonderfully Asian feeling, which, with some candles and incense, makes a nice space to meditate in. If you're really pushed for space, screening off a corner of your bedroom may do—you could build a small shrine (see page 46) and create a very personal, sacred space.

Breathe deeply

It is very easy to get into the habit of breathing badly. But good breathing is an essential chill-out technique. The way we breathe indicates how stressed we are. If we are relaxed, we breathe slowly and from the diaphragm. This is stomach breathing. It's very relaxing and good for us. When we are under pressure our breathing changes. It becomes shallow and rapid and moves upwards to our upper chest. We also tend to tense our stomachs, making stomach breathing much harder as the diaphragm gets restricted. Upper chest breathing has several side effects:

❖ *It causes the body to eliminate too much carbon dioxide, which makes the blood too alkaline.*
❖ *It causes the blood vessels in the brain to narrow, which slows the circulation of oxygen in the brain.*
❖ *It can cause palpitations, dizziness, chest pains, and panic attacks.*

Even if you think you are breathing properly, try the following exercise, which not only makes you aware of the way you breathe and how you can gain more control over it, but also calms you down.

❖ *Wear loose and comfortable clothing. Find somewhere quiet where you won't be disturbed. Sit upright on a dining chair.*
❖ *Place one hand on your chest and one hand on your stomach to feel whether you instinctively breathe from your upper chest or from your diaphragm.*
❖ *Listen to your breathing. Slowly breathe in and out through your nose only, ten times. If you can hear your breathing, you are doing it too heavily.*
❖ *Make an effort to breathe with your diaphragm. Make sure you can really feel your stomach rising and falling.*
❖ *Breathe in through your nose, for a count of five, and out through your mouth, for a count of ten. Repeat ten times. This will regulate your breathing.*
❖ *Make sure the breathing movement in your body is forward and back rather*

than up and down. Sit bolt upright and look straight ahead.

❖ *Allow a pause between each breath in and out. Do this ten times. You can silently mouth the word "relax" or "calm" to help you take the full pause.*

❖ *Finally, allow your body to relax naturally and let go of all tension.*

You can do these simple exercises whenever you begin to feel tense or notice that your breathing is becoming upper chest breathing rather than from your diaphragm. It takes a little practice, but you will soon find that every time you do the exercises you feel calmer. Eventually you will find you have conditioned yourself to be aware of your breathing at all times, which is of great benefit to your general health.

Transform a piece of junk

Painting old pieces of furniture is addictive. It will stimulate you, relax you, bring out your creative side, and give you something wonderful to show at the end of it. Your labors will be rewarded and your creative talents praised. And you will have done some hard work, enjoyed yourself, and been so busy your cares and worries will have mysteriously dropped away.

PAINT EFFECTS

To create a crackle glaze, first paint the piece of furniture and then apply a crackle glaze mixture—available from craft stores—over the top. As it dries it "crackles" into thin lines, creating an elegant aged effect.

Try scumbling. This involves applying a thick layer of paint over a painted surface in thin lines, like imitation wood. You can buy a scumbling comb, but an ordinary comb does just as good a job. Paint the wood and let it dry. Paint over it in another color and drag the comb through the wet paint before it dries to expose the different color underneath.

You can make a piece of furniture look like a family heirloom by "weathering" it. This is achieved by applying many layers of paint and sanding down each coat to expose the paint underneath. Begin with a single coat of white paint. When it is dry, lightly rub it with a candle. The wax will prevent the next coat of paint from adhering. Rub the wax into crevices and corners, but leave panels and flat surfaces. Paint the item again in a second color. Leave to dry. Again rub with the wax, but this time leave the crevices and corners untouched, and wax only the panels and flat surfaces. Apply another coat of paint with a third color. Leave to dry completely—several days if possible. Now you can attack it with sandpaper. Rub all the corners to expose the paint underneath, and in certain areas the paint underneath that as well. You'll find that where the wax was applied the paint has either not adhered or rubs off very easily indeed. You will be left with a piece of wooden furniture that looks beautifully rustic and weathered.

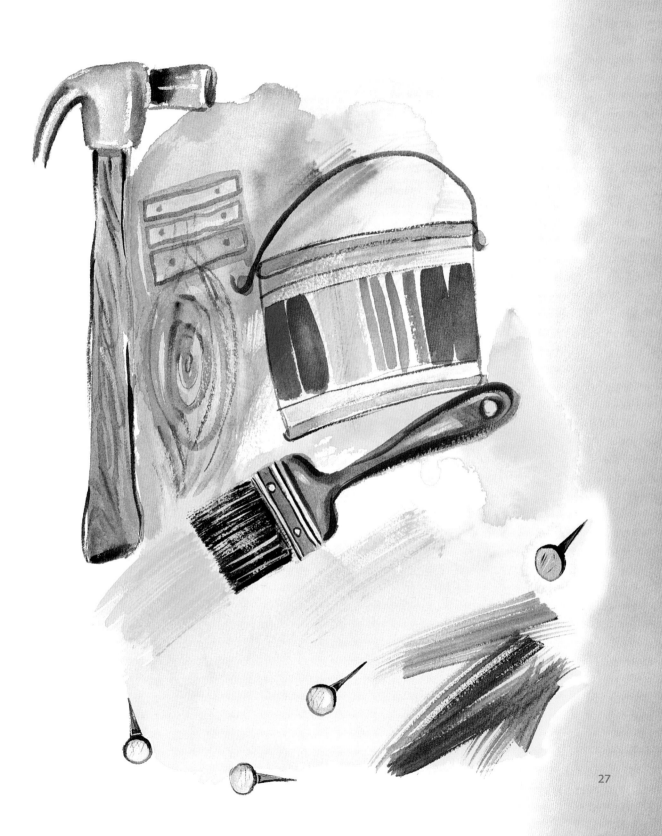

Grow an orchard in a pot

By creating an orchard in a pot we gain some control over nature. If you are ever feeling overwhelmed by life's events, try growing an orchard in a pot and see how much better it makes you feel.

By growing our own tiny orchard we are reminded that nature has rhythms and seasons, times of plenty and times of drought. The same is true of our own lives. By seeing this in miniature, we come to appreciate that whatever our situation is, it will change. If we have bare branches now, in a season or two we will be in full leaf.

WHICH FRUITS?

To create a lush, fruity, miniature orchard, first you need seeds. You can buy these from a garden center or nursery—follow the germination instructions on the packet—but it is more fun to find your own seeds in pieces of organic fruit.

You can grow trees from the seeds of apples, pears, lemons, oranges, melons, avocados, or kiwi fruit. Any fruit you can find in the farmers' market could yield a good result. Try pomegranates for a truly exotic orchard. You don't even have to limit yourself to just one type of tree—try mixing several unusual trees together in your orchard and see how pleasing the results can be.

CREATING THE ORCHARD

Remember how when you were a child you grew seeds wrapped in paper towels and soaked in water? It's still the best way of germinating fruit seeds. Place the seeds and paper towels in a jar, and make sure the water gets topped up regularly and that it gets lots of natural light. Alternatively, you could plant your seeds in potting compost, a technique which usually yields very quick results.

Check daily to see whether your seeds have sprouted, then transplant them into a pot. Then, much like ourselves, all your orchard needs to flourish is tender, loving care.

Create a collage

Want to create some imaginative pictures? Let's raid the pantry. Pasta shapes come in all shapes and sizes and can be glued onto backing card. Create shapes and pictures with them using the different colors and textures. You can use plain pasta and paint it when you've finished gluing it.

How about a 3-D effect? You could use a shallow glass dish and pour the pasta shapes in and see how they intermingle and create unusual pictures by themselves. Or pour them into a long, thin glass jar. How about using dried fruit?

Or cake decorations? You can make lots of colorful and unusual collages.

FINDING MATERIALS

Go outside and use leaves, dried flowers and grasses, bark, pebbles, lichen, moss—whatever you can find. Inside you can use fabric, paper, photographs, egg boxes, colored paper, glass marbles—even paper clips.

Creating a collage from unusual materials is relaxing and stimulating at the same time—once you get started, your imagination will know no bounds.

Treat someone you love to a manicure or pedicure

We are humans and we need to be in close physical contact with other humans. If we still lived in a more primitive but natural way we would groom each other. The conventions of civilization mean we no longer groom each other, but by giving a loved one a manicure or pedicure we are grooming, being kind, getting to know our partner in a very intimate but nonsexual way, staying in touch, and reassuring them we love them.

A manicure is care of the hands and a pedicure is care of the feet. Some people's feet are too ticklish to touch but everyone loves having their hand held.

MANICURE

Start by oiling and massaging the hands. Stroke the hands in a loving way. Cut the fingernails and smooth the edges with a light emery board. Use a blunt wooden stick to lightly push back the cuticles.

PEDICURE

Care of bunions and corns is best left to a podiatrist, but you can cut the nails and massage them in the same way you would for a manicure.

31

Be at one with the elements

We are born of the wind and the rain and the sun. If we are cut off from nature, we are distanced from our true selves. Without contact with the elements, we live in an artificial world, spending too much time working and not enough time reacquainting ourselves with where we really come from.

By being at one with the elements we reconnect with nature, with the seasons, with real life. In some cultures this is a form of religion. The word religion means to rebind, to rebind ourselves to nature and the universe. The more relaxed and chilled out we are the more we are in contact with our natural, elemental selves.

HOW DO WE RECONNECT WITH NATURE?

First of all we have to recognize the elements—sun, rain, wind, and snow— and that these are represented by fire, water, air, and earth. By lighting a bonfire we invoke the healing powers of the sun (see page 52). By lighting a stick of incense we summon the wind in the smoke. By pouring water we emulate the rain. And by collecting stones we can hold in our hands the age-old spirit of the earth.

We can use these elements within elements to build a shrine (see page 46) to the powerful forces of nature that have shaped and molded our lives.

DANCING IN THE RAIN

We carry umbrellas in case it rains, we cover ourselves with sunscreen to prevent sunburns, we dread the snow in case we can't get to work, and we won't go out in a thunderstorm in case we get struck by lightning. It's time to forget our cares and dance in the rain. It might even be time to throw off our clothes and *really* get back to nature.

Make a bird table

Watching birds feed is so natural, so relaxing, and so endearing that we cannot help but smile and feel better.

You can make a bird table by attaching a flat, square, board to a high pole, then sinking the pole into the ground. Scatter food on the board and the birds will soon come to feed. A bird table should be raised up off the ground, should have a steep central pole with the feeder overhanging it so cats can't climb it, and should be located in the open so the birds can escape easily if they are threatened.

If you live in an apartment, put out food on your windowsill for the birds. You can buy wire feeders that hang up or attach to the glass of the window with little rubber suction cups. Fill these feeders with nuts and seeds.

You can also hang a wooden box up on chains from a tree and fill it with food. You can raise and lower it so it's easy to replenish. And once your feathered friends flock to your table, you will experience hours of absorbed relaxation!

Start a family newsletter

If you're lucky enough to have a family who supports you when you need it, remember to include them when things go well, too. Start a family newsletter as a chill-out technique. They get to contribute, and you get the fun of editing it.

If you have a computer, your newsletter can be produced with a word processing program, or you could even handwrite it for a truly personal feel. It isn't expensive to make a few copies at your local copy shop. However you choose to put your newsletter together, here are some tips:

POINTERS FOR EDITORS

To make your newsletter look attractive and accessible, make sure the layout is clean, with lots of white space. Try using bullet points for legibility and impact. For example:

❖ *WHERE: Auntie May's house*

❖ *WHEN: Friday 26 August, 8pm*

❖ *WHY: Bob's birthday*

Ask everyone to contribute—that means the children as well. They can write about what they are learning at school and what they're doing for the holidays. Get the younger ones to draw pictures of family members—they can be scanned into your computer if you are using one. Older ones could write more sophisticated articles. Include a digest of family news and events, a well-loved recipe or two, a family tree, or a brief account of the family's history or how its name came about.

Edit long, rambling articles to shorter, snappier ones that are more interesting and readable. Don't try to cram too much in—better to save things for the next issue than make your newsletter look too busy.

Your newsletter can be recorded on tape for those whose eyesight isn't as good as it was, and it's cheap and easy to email it to family overseas.

A family newsletter brings people together. It's simple, inexpensive, and lots of fun. It makes everyone feel cared about and that they belong.

Be a photographer

How we see the world depends on how we view ourselves. If we are gloomy, the world looks bleak. If we are upbeat and cheerful, the world is a brighter place. But the opposite is also true. If we see the world as a magical place, we cannot help but become magical people. If we think the world is dark and unhelpful, how can we be happy?

Photography is a useful way of turning our view of the world upside down. If before we saw things as gray and dull, we can change that image by playing with visual imagery via photography. Taking pictures encompasses art, creativity, visual appreciation, taking time to really look at the world, being absorbed, being stimulated, and, above all, changing our perception of what is around us. All you need is a camera—and it doesn't have to be a sophisticated one. Just a "point-and-shoot" is enough. Remember, this isn't about technical prowess and expensive equipment, but about the way you perceive the world and the surprising and beautiful things you can find in it. Here are some ideas:

❖ *Spot striking, unexpected juxtapositions of colors, such as a pink cherry blossom that has fallen onto a shiny, blue car hood, or two contrasting plates stacked on your kitchen shelf.*

❖ *Photograph things from unusual angles, or objects that are reflected in a mirror or window.*

❖ *Capture the beauty of people's faces in the glow of candlelight or a bonfire.*

❖ *Stand on a hill and turn through 360 degrees, taking a picture every thirty degrees or so—you'll get an amazing panoramic view.*

❖ *Try making a photographic record of your face over a year—take a new photo every morning. When the year is up, look back over your photographs and see how you have changed.*

❖ *Take a photo of a favorite view once a week for a year and watch how the seasons change it.*

These ideas are only the start—the only limits are those of your own imagination! Photography can be a relaxing and rewarding hobby in so many ways.

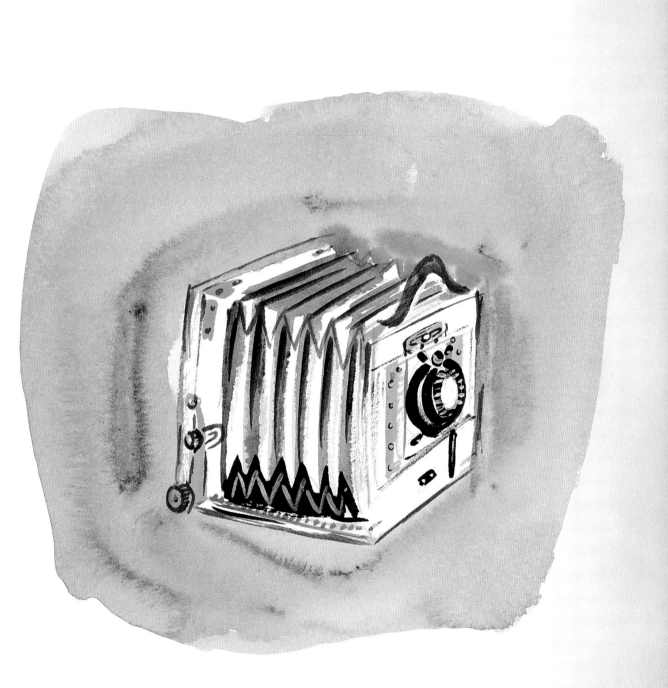

Find an amulet

An amulet is a personal lucky charm. You can keep it in your pocket or around your neck and touch it whenever you need comfort. Your amulet has amazing powers: it can inspire you with confidence and suffuse your soul with a wonderful feeling of well-being.

To make an amulet, you need a small object that means something to you, that has some power to you personally. It has to be something small so it can be carried about on your person. It might be a pebble with a hole in it that you picked up on the beach or a toy from your childhood. I have a lucky keyring made out of a metal toy car from the 1950s. You could use a rosary or a favorite photo of a beloved friend or family member in a tiny case. How about a whistle or a tiny doll?

Lots of people use an amulet—a favorite keyring or pendant—but they wouldn't recognize it as such. It's still a good luck charm when carried about the person all day and used for comfort and reassurance.

Mix your own muesli

A good breakfast gives vitality, and fills us with essential vitamins and minerals. Muesli is full of all the things we need to feel really alive. It contains protein, carbohydrates, sugars, fiber, sodium, and potassium. Contribute to the "you are what you eat" philosophy in a very real way by making your own. To make muesli, simply combine in a bowl a selection of the ingredients in the panel on the right. It is good served with milk, soy milk, rice milk, or sprinkled on yogurt.

INGREDIENTS

Rolled oats

Rolled barley

Rolled wheat

Wheat germ

Millet

Alfalfa seeds

Poppy seeds

Sesame seeds

Sunflower seeds

Rolled rice

Puffed corn

Dried apples, banana chips, papayas, pears, mangos

Coconut

A little honey

Almonds

Raisins, currants, dates

Walk with awareness

As our lives get busier and more hectic, we start to rush everything we do. This rushing leads us to walk with our heads permanently bent forward as we fly headlong to our next appointment or meeting. We become very goal-oriented and lose touch with a simpler, more chilled way of life.

YOU ARE HOW YOU WALK

No one expects you to drop those meetings or cancel your appointments and go off and live on a desert island. We can't dismiss reality with all its pressures. Instead we have to work with it and learn new responses.

Clinical trials have shown that body posture and mental state are very closely interconnected. Similarly, an open, head-up body placement is reflected in an open personality—optimistic and cheerful. A closed, head-down body placement is often reflected in a depressed outlook. Walking with awareness not only improves your

posture but also allows you to look around—and enjoy it. And it doesn't make your progress any slower—in fact, your walking may even become faster as it takes on a new efficiency.

NOTICING THREE THINGS

Next time you walk down the road, to your car, or to the office—or any regular short walk you take—try looking for three things you haven't noticed before along the route. These things might be flowers in a garden, trees overhanging your path, a carving above a door, an unusual roofline, the color of a window, the texture of the sidewalk, or the way the light changes as you enter a building. Try noticing three new things each time you take the same walk and be aware of what is going on around you at all times. It won't slow you down, but it will make it more relaxing because you'll be looking around you instead of thinking ahead to your lunch, your meeting, going home, or being on time. This is called walking with awareness. And it has fitness benefits too. Once your head comes up to look around, your whole body lengthens and becomes more upright. You take in more oxygen and use less energy.

BODY AWARENESS

It is surprisingly easy and very helpful to be aware of the movements of your body as well as of the outside world. As you walk, imagine there is a piece of string attached to the top of your head that is pulling you very gently upright. Each time you are tempted to look down, hunch your shoulders, or droop your head, remember the string and allow yourself to be pulled upright. Your walking posture will improve, you'll breathe better, and you'll be more relaxed. Once your posture improves, so does your mental outlook—you'll not only look more relaxed, alert, and efficient, but you'll become so mentally as well. It really works!

Make home-made jam

Spring rain and summer sun bring forth a rich bounty from the earth, good fruit we can enjoy—the harvest of the hedgerows. Relax and enjoy making homemade jam to spread on the bread you've baked (see page 60). There is nothing more soothing on a winter's day than opening a pot of homemade jam and smelling the fruit, tasting its richness, and unlocking the sunshine.

Jam-making is relaxing in three wonderful ways—picking the fruit, making the jam and, finally, enjoying it. There is a special joy in wandering down a pretty country lane on a summer day, picking blackberries, eating a few as you go, enjoying the sun, and smelling the clean, fresh air.

Jam-making has gone on unchanged for hundreds of years. You can follow the same basic recipe your great-great-grandparents would have used, and enjoy the same juicy results. Try one of these three delicious suggestions. Take your time and enjoy!

RASPBERRY JAM

Pick about 4 pounds of raspberries. Rub the inside of a saucepan with butter and place the fruit into it. In a separate pan, warm an equal amount of sugar. Heat the berries until they start to boil, and then pour in the warm sugar. Stir the mixture vigorously for about 20 minutes and then leave to cool. Pour into jars, seal, and store in a cool, dark place.

THREE-FRUIT JAM

Pick 2 pounds each of apples, pears, and plums. Peel, core, and slice the apples and pears. Stone the plums. In a saucepan, cook all the fruit with 24 ounces of water until it is soft. In a separate pan, warm 1 pound of sugar. Add the warmed sugar and the grated rind of a lemon to the fruit mixture. Bring to a boil and keep boiling until all the sugar is dissolved—this should take about 10 minutes. Leave to cool. Pour into jars, seal, and store in a cool, dark place.

BLACKBERRY AND APPLE JAM

Pick 2 pounds of blackberries and 2 pounds of sour apples. Wash the berries and peel, core, and slice the apples. Put the fruit into a pan with 8 ounces of water and cook until tender—this should take about 20 minutes. Add 3 pounds of sugar and stir until dissolved. Bring to a boil and keep boiling until the jam sets. Cool, pour into jars, seal, and store in a cool, dark place.

Make angel cards

Deep within us we have the intuitive understanding to know exactly what we need to live in a more relaxed way and achieve a more chilled way of life. We need to find a way of drawing that understanding up from those hidden depths. By using angel cards, we can give our subconscious mind something to focus on, which helps us acquire this vital information from within ourselves.

To make angel cards, decorate the back of a sheet of card stock with colored pens—put all your creativity into it— and then cut it up into small pieces two inches long by half-an-inch wide. On each card write a key word from the list on the opposite page. Substitute your own personal words if you want to.

To use your angel cards, choose three cards at random. Each key word should spark something in you when you read it. The first tells you which quality you need to develop. The second card tells you which quality you should share with others. The third tells you which quality should soon be coming your way.

Find or make a bag for your cards and dip into them every morning to discover what the day has in store.

KEY WORDS

✳

compassion ✳ imagination ✳ abundance
morality ✳ tenderness ✳ encouragement
optimism ✳ simplicity ✳ openness
wisdom ✳ emotion ✳ charisma ✳ delight
playfulness ✳ strength ✳ independence
harmony ✳ contentment ✳ enhancement
purity ✳ spontaneity ✳ responsibility
exhilaration ✳ communication
enthusiasm ✳ reasonableness
understanding ✳ integrity ✳ enjoyment
adventure ✳ grace ✳ love ✳ spirituality
importance ✳ creativity ✳ clarity
freedom ✳ kindness ✳ surrender
practicality ✳ courage ✳ self-improvement
humor ✳ inspiration ✳ empowerment
refinement ✳ nurture ✳ faith
flexibility ✳ joy ✳ purpose ✳ forgiveness
patience ✳ engagement ✳ release
honesty ✳ gratitude ✳ happiness
pleasantness ✳ expectancy

Build a shrine

A shrine is a focus for our spiritual needs and aspirations. It should occupy the center of our home—and the center of our hearts. A shrine is important whatever our spiritual direction and beliefs. It crystallizes our feelings and thoughts in a very real and tangible way.

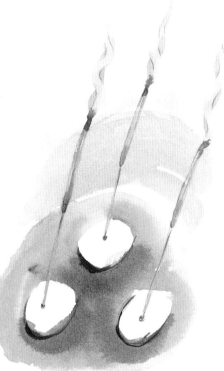

WHAT TO USE

Some religious practices have established icons such as statues and holy objects that you can use in creating your shrine. But if you follow a looser, less organized belief system, use objects that are personal to you. Try gathering treasures from nature to focus your meditations and prayers on. Driftwood, pebbles, and shells echo the sea. Mossy wood, acorns, and feathers call to us from the woods. Stones and metal sing to us of the earth. The smoke from incense draws our thoughts upwards to the sky and the heavens.

CREATING YOUR SHRINE

All you need is a low table covered with a rich, beautiful fabric. Place the objects you have gathered in a pleasing arrangement. Add some color and decoration—perhaps with favorite inspiring photographs or postcards. Add a few crystals and a candle floating in a bowl of pure spring water.

USING YOUR SHRINE

You don't need to do anything. Just be there once or twice a day and allow your shrine to speak to you. Let it inspire you, transform you, uplift you, and focus you. You can use the time to sit quietly in meditation or in prayer.

Write your life story in 25 words or fewer

This is a chill-out technique with a deeper side. It combines the fun of creativity with the opportunity to confront your own life and examine where changes need to be made.

PUT PEN TO PAPER

Think hard for a while about how your life has gone so far. Put your immediate thoughts and feelings into simple and direct words—twenty-five or fewer. There are no other rules. You don't even have to write in sentences. This isn't about jotting down a list of achievements or problems, but instead an exercise to get you thinking. Think about who you are and how far you have come. Try to sum up the important points.

When, as in this exercise, you are forced to be concise and succinct, you will find that the real truths of your life come shining through. You can then take steps to make any changes and improvements that need to be made.

EXAMPLES

Forgiving friend. Lover. Poet.
Searched for answers. Found some.
Took to the sea. Traveled the world.
Came home. Still searching.
(twenty words)

❖

I was born a woman but think
like a man. I fight hard and play often.
I dance in the sun and
celebrate my life.
(twenty-five words)

❖

Born. Grew. Lived. Loved. Lost and
found. Reunited and joyful. Served my
country. Growing old in peace.
Happy now.
(nineteen words)

Try yoga

The more supple and fit we are, the suppler and fitter our mental attitude is. Yoga is effective for countless millions of people across the world. It's very chilled. You don't get out of breath or have to visit the gym. You can do it in the safety and privacy of your own home. It is a languid form of exercise designed to relax you and get you fit without you even noticing. It keeps you young and healthy, and once you begin to experience its benefits, it rapidly becomes part of your everyday routine.

Yoga is a series of basic movements designed to stretch and exercise every part of your body. They often resemble the movements animals make. Ever seen a cat working out in a gym? They don't need to. They stretch.

GUIDELINES
❖ *Ask a doctor's advice before starting yoga if you have back problems, high blood pressure, or are pregnant.*
❖ *Wear loose, comfortable clothes.*
❖ *Ease yourself into positions gently.*
❖ *Relax and breathe evenly.*
❖ *Practice regularly, ideally for at least 10 minutes a day.*
❖ *Don't force yourself into awkward, uncomfortable positions.*

WHEN?
You can practice yoga whenever you wish. However, some people find it difficult to sleep if they practice immediately before going to bed. Try practicing

comfortable for you—this is about relaxation, not about making you more stressed trying to fit in your yoga sessions around other commitments!

WHERE?

It is preferable to practice yoga in a room that isn't too hot or cold. During warm weather, it is blissful to practice outside in the garden or even in a secluded spot in the park. The surface you practice on should be soft but firm—if a gym mat is not available, a folded blanket will do just as well.

GETTING STARTED

Set aside a few minutes to sit or lie quietly and clear your mind before starting the stretches and postures. The following simple program starts gently and then progresses on to more complex and demanding postures.

first thing in the morning or in the early evening, before eating. Yoga appears to be more successful if you set aside regular times to practice rather than haphazardly trying to fit it into your life.

EASY POSTURE

Sit with both knees bent and your feet on the floor. Bring your feet back and tuck them in front of your thighs so

HOW OFTEN?

To be most successful, yoga needs to be practiced for one hour at least three times a week. However, do whatever is

chill out

your toes point in opposite directions. Straighten your spine, lift your chest, and press the lower spine slightly forward. Rest your hands on your knees or let them meet and rest on your thighs.

LOTUS POSTURE

From a sitting position, rest the right foot on the left thigh, near the hip joint, and the left foot on the right thigh, also near the hip joint. Clench your jaws. Press your tongue against the roof of your mouth.

This is thought to be the best posture for meditation. The loop seals the prana—the vital breath of the body—enabling you to reach a more profound level of consciousness.

YOGA POSTURE

Sit cross-legged on the floor. Put your hands behind you and grip your left wrist with your right hand. Draw in a deep breath, lean forward, and slowly bring your forehead and nose into contact with the floor. Exhale as you lower your head. Keep your head on the floor for about eight seconds, then rise up slowly, breathing in as you reach your original position.

GREAT GOD POSTURE

Kneel down and sit on your heels. Bend your toes downwards, pointing backwards. Lift your chest, stretch your arms towards your knees, and rest the backs of your hands against your thighs, your fingers pointing towards your groin. Look down at an imaginary point directly on the tip of your nose.

FISH POSTURE

Lie down on your back with your legs in the lotus posture. Throw your arms behind your head and grasp each shoulder with the opposite hand. Allow your head to rest on your forearms.

This is an excellent, relaxing stretch for the shoulders, and the cervical and lumbar regions of your spine.

DRAWN BOW POSTURE

Lie flat, face downward. Bend
your knees, reach behind,
and grasp your ankles. Raise
your head, chest, and legs to
form an arch. Extend your neck
and chest as far as you can.
Breathe in while raising your
body and hold for eight
seconds. Exhale as you return
to your starting position.

LOCUST POSTURE

Lie down flat, face downward.
Place your arms on your sides and
stretch your hands backward, palms
facing up. Rest your chin on the floor.
Raise your legs and waist with your fists
clenched. Hold for thirty seconds.

SQUEEZE POSTURE

Lie on your back. Bend your right knee
and bring your thigh to your chest.
Grasp your leg with both hands. Keep
this position for eight seconds, holding
your breath, then exhale and let go.
Repeat with the other leg.

Build a bonfire

I have a childhood memory of a man tending a bonfire late on a summer evening while whistling "Moon River." He was wreathed in smoke and silhouetted against the red, dusky sky. It is a memory that haunts me in a delicious way. That bonfire lit over 40 years ago is still burning, still inspiring, still evocative and stirring.

WHY A BONFIRE?

Lighting our own bonfire stirs something in us, makes us one with nature. We poke and prod, pile on twigs, add a few leaves, watch the smoke chase us around, smell the delicious wood scents, and feel rejuvenated and recharged. We get smoky and covered in ash. We stand and dream as we watch the licking flames. A bonfire does something to all of us that is deeply moving. Building a bonfire satisfies that part of us that still lives in caves and hunts across a grassy plain. It brings out the nomad, the hunter, and the primitive child of our past.

BE CONSIDERATE

Don't light a bonfire when your neighbors have just hung out their washing or are sitting enjoying the summer air in the garden. Tell them when you plan one so they can shut their windows.

Watch out for the safety of small children—they are just as fascinated as you are but a little less experienced. Only burn garden waste such as woody stems, cuttings, and leaves. Don't burn plastic or household rubbish. A bonfire is perhaps best kept for the fall when you need to get rid of cleared leaves.

Collect stones

Stones aren't just stones. They are tangible records of the past. They are solid representations of nature, weather, and the forces of the universe. Each one is unique. Stones speak to us of the passing of time and the wearing away of the hardest substances. Stones are solid and reliable. They endure.

LEAVING PAIN BEHIND

If you experience anything bad in a place, select a stone to leave behind. Choose one that represents—by its shape or color or texture, weight, or composition—what you've been through. Into it pour out your troubles and leave all that stuff behind when you leave. The stone will slowly

Each time you go to a special place, old or new, bring back a single stone to remind you of your experiences. Keep the stone, and it will summon up the essence of your adventures better than any photograph. It is a lasting reminder of the place itself, as well as of your impressions and what you understood about the place.

leach the pain back into the earth. Likewise, take a stone with you to purify yourself on a journey. Choose a beautiful stone, one that is full of joy and light.

Over time your stone collection will grow and each one will bring back memories, rekindle your awareness of special places, and speak to you in its own earthy tongue.

chill out

Be your own beauty therapist

Massaging your own face and head can be enormously relaxing and beneficial for health and beauty alike. Choose somewhere quiet and make sure you are warm enough. Sit on a comfortable chair or lie on the floor. Make sure you have plenty of time as you don't want to rush this. Use a little light carrier oil, which is usually used in aromatherapy (see page 12) if you wish.

STAGE 1

❖ *Close your eyes. Using the flat of your hands, start to stroke your face gently. Stroke from the center of your forehead out to the temples. Do this three times. Then stroke from the center of your nose out to your cheek-bones—again three times. Next, stroke three times from the center of your mouth out along your jawline.*

❖ *Use your three middle fingers to circle your face all over, pressing firmly. Feel for any areas of tension and spend the most time on these.*

❖ *Use your thumbs and forefingers to gently squeeze and pull on your ear-lobes. Do the same all around the tops and edges of your ears.*

❖ *Place your hands flat over your ears and press hard until you can't hear anything except the "sound of the sea." Stay like this for a moment or two. Relax and enjoy.*

❖ *Use the pads of your fingers to tap very gently under your eyes and over your eyelids.*

STAGE 2

❖ *Place the palms of your hands on your temples and rest your fingertips on the top of your head. Make small circular movements with your fingertips, using firm pressure, over as much of your head as you can reach.*

❖ *Staying in the same position, gently massage the front and sides of your head, including your temples, eye sockets, cheeks, and chin, with the heels of your hands.*

❖ *Run your hands through your hair and gently tug on the roots as you go. Do this several times.*

STAGE 3

❖ *Imagine lines radiating from your nose across your whole face about one inch apart. Work along these lines, pressing gently with your forefingers every half an inch. Work up from the nose to the forehead, across the cheeks and under the eyes, down under the cheek bones, along the jaw line, and finally down the mouth and under the chin.*

❖ *It's very likely that you could be asleep by now! If not, stay where you are for a moment and enjoy the feeling of utter relaxation that comes from this kind of self-pampering.*

Plant a tree

Seasons come and go, and sometimes we need to mark their passage to feel rooted in the earth and a part of nature. We celebrate births and deaths by sending cards but sometimes a natural, more permanent celebration is needed. Planting a tree to mark a special occasion is an old tradition but one that has fallen out of fashion. It's time to resurrect it!

Plant a tree when a child is born—it is then that child's tree, its growth equates with the child's, its seasons with his or her rhythms, and its strength with the child's strength. You can bury the placenta under the roots as a natural and emotional fertilizer.

Marriage also can be celebrated by planting a tree—the couple make a joint pledge to look after their tree in the same way they look after each other.

WHAT TREES TO PLANT?

Choose the tree to suit the occasion and the space available. If you only have a tiny backyard, then it is short-sighted to plant a horse chestnut, as it will eventually take over your whole yard. Fruit trees are productive and attractive but relatively short-lived.

To plant a tree, dig a hole slightly larger than its root ball and put growing compost in the bottom of it. Put your tree in and pack it in well. Water the tree a lot to begin with and protect from frost and intense heat.

Go jump roping

If you want exercise, fun, and lots of laughter then take up jump roping. It's a tremendous way to get fit and at the same time really enjoy yourself. Skipping rope requires coordination, which makes it very good for keeping us both mentally alert and physically agile. It has many different forms and methods and is usually done in one spot. All you need is a jump rope.

Before you can move onto more complex maneuvers, you need to be conversant with the basic technique.

Stand with your feet together, the handles of the jump rope in your hands, and the rope trailing on the ground behind you. Throw the rope over your head and, at the same time, get ready to jump over the rope as it passes under your feet—a little hop will suffice to begin with. Once you are really good and can skip fast, twist the rope as it comes over your head, alternate the foot you use to jump with, or try jumping rope backwards.

It's fun to jump your stresses away!

Papier mâché

Papier mâché is simple to make and a natural product that involves no complicated tools or expensive materials. It's a good medium to work with if you want to make a sculpture (see page 153) or a ritual mask (see page 153).

Working with your hands is relaxing and therapeutic. It absorbs you and while you are busy your mind gets a chance to switch off. Making papier mâché can be seen as a very messy form of meditation.

WHAT YOU NEED

Water	Poster paint
Lots of newspaper	White flour

Begin by tearing the newspaper into strips about one inch wide. Just doing this is good for getting rid of built-up aggression. Mix the flour and water in a large bowl—start with about three cups of each—until you have a gloppy, smooth paste. Have a shape ready (see ideas below). Dip a strip of newspaper into the paste and, as you take it out,

remove the excess paste with your fingers. Lay this strip on the shape and smooth out any wrinkles. Dip another strip and continue until the shape is covered. Leave to dry and then paint it.

MOOD MASK

You will need a sheet of heavy-duty aluminum foil. Mold it to your face, making sure you press it in well around your eyes, chin, mouth, and nose. Peel off very carefully. Stuff the inside of your mold with old newspaper to give it some backing strength. Cover the front with thin strips of papier mâché. Work it into the correct shape. Leave to dry. Paint your mask in colors to suit your mood: bright colors and patterns to reflect a happy mood, dark colors if you are depressed. Paint your mask half white and half black if you want to represent your light and dark sides. Make a different mask for every mood!

GIFT BALL

This project combines the relaxation of creativity and the joy of giving to others.

You will need a balloon. Blow it up, cover it in thin strips of papier mâché, and leave to dry. When it is fully dry, use a sharp knife to cut a slot in it which is big enough for your gift to fit through. This will puncture the balloon, which you can then retrieve through the slot.

Put your gift through the slot. Then reseal the slot with more papier mâché. Leave to dry and then paint the ball. Present this colourful surprise to a loved one, and watch them look confused as they try to work out how they are supposed to get at their gift.

Bake your own bread

Baking bread has three terrific benefits. First, the smell wafting through your home will remind you of childhood and security, warmth and love, and simplicity and freedom from the cares of the outside world. The smell of baking bread induces relaxation and euphoria.

Second, kneading bread releases anxiety and stress—pounding and rolling the dough kneads out all that pent-up aggression and tension. Kneading involves tensing and relaxing muscles which, when you are stressed, eases tension and helps you to relax. Making bread is productive, as well as wonderfully relaxing—much better than doing an exercise routine or simply punching a pillow.

And third, all that hot fresh bread has to be shared—invite a friend or two. Baking bread has gone on since the dawn of time—what better way to relax than sharing this tradition with your social circle.

Bread making is satisfying, stress-reducing, and sustaining. As you knead the dough, feel the tension leaving you.

As you smell the bread baking, close your eyes, breathe deeply, and relax. As you eat the hot, fresh bread, chew slowly and give thanks for such wonderful and simple pleasures.

WHAT YOU NEED

$1\frac{1}{2}$ pounds whole wheat flour

$1\frac{1}{2}$ pounds white flour

4 level teaspoons salt (optional)

1 level teaspoon brown sugar

$1\frac{3}{4}$ pints mixed milk and lukewarm water

1 teaspoon honey

2 ounces yeast

You will also need four standard-sized baking pans. This recipe makes four good-sized loaves, so make sure you invite lots of friends to your house to share them with.

Put the flour, salt, and sugar into a warm bowl and leave in a warm place. In a warm bowl, whisk the milk-water mixture with the honey and yeast. Add to the flour, mix with your hands to a stiff dough.

Now comes the kneading stage. This is best done on a floured board. Fold the dough over on itself and repeatedly push down with a firm, rocking motion until it becomes smooth and shiny. Do this for ten minutes. As you knead, feel the tension draining out of your body.

Divide the dough into four pieces, and shape to fit the bread pans. Grease the pans and half fill each one, press down firmly with damp fingers, cover with a damp cloth and let rise in a warm place until the dough has filled the tins. One rising period is enough as you are using whole wheat flour. This takes about 30 minutes.

At the end of the rising period, remove the cloth, brush the tops with milk or melted butter, and bake in a hot oven for about 25 minutes, or until done, at 450 degrees. Turn the loaves out of the tins and tap the bottoms. If they sound hollow, the bread is done. If not, take out of the tins, put back into the oven directly onto the shelf, and cook for five more minutes. Cool the loaves slightly on a wire rack. Slice and enjoy the bread while still warm.

Grow a bonsai tree

You can't control the universe and turn it to your way of thinking, but you can certainly control a tiny part of it. When you grow bonsai, that tiny part is nature—tamed to perfection. Bonsai is a useful therapeutic tool for those of us who sometimes feel the need to be more in control—it's helpful to have our own, very special bit of the natural world under our care and stewardship.

WHAT IS BONSAI?

Bonsai is the art of miniaturizing trees and shrubs. It began in Japan and has spread throughout the world. Bonsai trees take many, many years to reach perfection. Some in Japan are well over two hundred years old. Bonsai trees are not just small trees, but miniaturized replicas of trees that have been shaped by the powerful forces of nature.

SHORT CUTS

If you look in a wild part of your garden you will find small saplings that have self-seeded. Carefully dig them up. Trim the roots until you have a small root ball roughly a third of the size of the above-ground part of the tree. These roots need to be pruned from time to time to keep the tree small. Take off any normal-sized leaves and pot the tree in a flat-bottomed pot with a shallow lip. Use potting compost and water very sparingly. These saplings usually begin to grow immediately but you need quite a few to end up with one or two really good specimens. Keep them out of wind and rain. Make sure you've got permission if you take them from anywhere other than your own property.

A RELAXING THERAPY

You can spend hours training your tree. Use very thin wire to wrap around the branches to create the twisted, tortured shapes the wind and rain would forge on a full-sized tree. The tree will eventually grow into the shapes you have formed. Go to a garden center that stocks bonsai and study how the experts do it. You need only a few basic tools—a spoon and fork will do to begin with, plus a small pair of scissors.

Creating the wind-blasted shapes of a pine tree with its roots gripping a single huge rock, or a miniature stand of oak trees stunted by frosts and gales, can be fascinating. You need patience and imagination to visualize how the tree will end up. Go out into the countryside and see how nature shapes trees on a grand scale. You can then go home and recreate what you have seen in miniature.

TAKING CARE OF BONSAI

Bonsai need sunshine and fresh air as much as bigger trees do. The Japanese take them outside on sunny days and bring them in again in the evening to protect them from frost and bugs. Keep them out of direct sunlight, which can scorch the leaves. This is not an instant hobby—but with perseverance you can create something of real beauty.

Decorate your hands with henna

Mehndi is an ancient Eastern tradition of ritualistic ornamentation to celebrate betrothal, marriage, or birth. It puts you in touch with a simpler, more natural way of life and encourages community spirit. As you paint with your henna brush, you tap into an intuitive and spiritual creativity passed down through the centuries.

It is used on both men and women. In India women henna their friends to celebrate festivals. Henna is a skin dye, not a permanent tattoo. It stains the skin reddish-brown, lasts for several weeks, and is harmless as long as you use green (not black) henna.

Buy fresh henna powder that smells richly fragrant from a cosmetic store. Avoid stale henna, which is odorless and stains a very pale orange. Sift the henna to remove any impurities such as plant stalks or twigs and mix the refined powder with a little lemon juice or lime juice to make a thick paste. Leave this to sit overnight. Thin it out with more juice until it is as runny as yogurt. Stir well to remove the lumps. You are now ready for painting.

You can get a more defined design by using a thin stick rather than a paintbrush. Draw the henna along your skin. If you've got the right consistency, the stick should leave a trail behind it. You can use a squeeze bottle but practice first on some paper. Leave the henna on for about six hours. To protect your henna design, wrap cling film around the skin or seal the henna by dabbing it with lemon juice and sugar. The hotter your skin gets the better the stain will take. After six hours, scrape off the green henna paste to reveal a beautiful orange-brown design.

Whittle some wood

Wood whittling isn't done very often nowadays, which is a shame. It's very therapeutic and relaxing, and keeps your hands fit and supple, helping to prevent arthritis in the finger joints in later life.

You need a small, sharp penknife and a small piece of soft wood—this can even be a twig you found under a tree. All you need to do is shave little slivers of wood off the big piece. That's it. It's marvelously unproductive, and you'll find it can be tremendously addictive once you get into it.

You wind up with a small pile of shavings at your feet and no wood left in your hands. Sharpen the knife, get another piece of wood, and start again.

CUTTING WOOD AIMLESSLY

The dictionary definition of whittling is to pare or cut with a knife; to diminish gradually; to cut wood aimlessly. That's it. To cut wood aimlessly. What better way to spend a warm evening on the porch chatting with loved ones and enjoying a beer than by whittling a little wood?

Color your life

Want to change your life? Want to create the new you? Then change the colors around you. Go from drab to vibrant in an instant—physically and emotionally, spiritually and mentally. All you need is to know the colors, what they mean, and how to work with them.

Color colors every facet of our lives—from clothes to furniture, food, environment, and even mood. Who hasn't seen red, been green with envy, been in the pink of health, felt purple with indignation, turned white with shock, or had the blues?

Color affects our moods deeply. Rooms painted in pale blues can actually lower blood pressure and calm us down, whereas red rooms raise our blood pressure and excite us.

WHICH COLORS SUIT YOU?

What seasons do you like? If the answer's spring, chances are you like pale greens, yellows, and blues. Summer, and it's vibrant reds and pinks for you. Fall is browns, grays, and gold, and winter the darkest colors.

How about foods? People tend to go not only for taste and texture, but also the color of food as a preference.

What colors do you like to wear? Have you thought about why? Have a look in your wardrobe and see which colors predominate. These are the ones you have chosen to reflect your personality. If you want to make changes, start here. Throw out any that you think don't represent the new you.

COLOR BREATHING

Find somewhere comfortable to sit where you won't be disturbed. Close your eyes and concentrate on your breathing. Imagine yourself breathing in not only air but also colored light. Relax and allow it to be slow, natural, and rhythmic. With each intake of breath, imagine colored light entering your body and bringing with it health, relaxation, and warmth. With each breath out, imagine all the trouble and tension leaving your body forever. Focus on different colors to achieve the different qualities you want to bring into your life.

BLUE for truth, inspiration,
and higher wisdom

❊

GOLD for abundance

❊

GREEN for fertility, harmony,
and ease of suffering

❊

ORANGE for positive thinking

❊

PINK for love, healing, and friendship

❊

PURPLE for enhancing your psychic abilities

❊

RED for courage, sexual energy,
and strength

❊

SILVER for clairvoyance and intuition

❊

WHITE for purity and peace, tranquillity,
and the highest spiritual aspirations

❊

YELLOW for creativity
and good communication

Plan a themed meal for friends

Eating with friends can become a group chill-out experience. We all love dressing up and partying. You can combine the two to create an unusual theme party for your friends.

Just think up a theme and allow your imagination to take wing. Cook a meal that is in keeping with it. If you're not a keen cook, ask the guests to bring the food. There's no need to pay too much attention to formal seating arrangements or elaborate decor. The real fun is in the planning, in selecting the right theme—and in seeing how your friends will dress up to represent it.

Give your guests a very general sense of the meal's theme and allow them to make of it what they will—it's hugely entertaining to see how widely interpretations differ. Just give them a single word—for example Greek, romantic, literary, bizarre, sea, history, or magic—and see what wacky and inventive costumes they come up with.

Decorate a holy well

For generations, local country folk have decorated holy wells and water springs at ritual times of the year. This ancient custom predates Christianity. Wells have been venerated as places of pilgrimage and worship as far back as before the Bronze Age. Anywhere that water sprang from the ground as if by magic was regarded as holy. Many old stories exist about the healing powers of holy wells.

YOUR OWN HOLY WELL

Not everyone can live near a holy well. So why not make your own? A simple water feature, such as a spout of water falling into a tub or trough, can become a spiritual focus point in your garden. If you don't have an underground spring to harness, you can easily buy a simple pump-driven water feature from your local garden center.

You can venerate and use your holy well exactly as your ancestors did in ancient times. Scatter flowers and leaves on the water on New Year's morning to ensure good luck for the rest of the year. At the summer solstice (the longest day in the calendar year), decorate your well with fresh-cut flowers and floating candles. At Easter and the fall equinox, bring fresh fruit. By doing this you will be following traditions that date back to the birth of humanity. And, of course, the sound of running water is wonderfully relaxing.

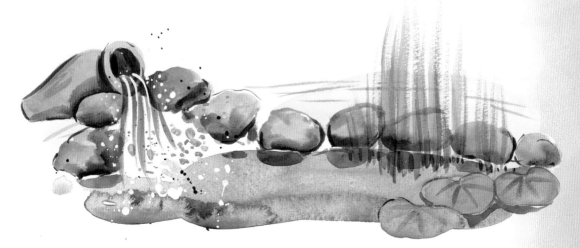

Take dancing lessons

Dancing has been found to be one of the most effective ways of combating stress. There is a whole range of dances to learn, from modern to jive, from Greek to circle dancing. Join a class, meet new friends, and learn a fun and extremely relaxing way to chill out.

WHY DANCE?

Tribal societies have long used dance as a way of expressing feelings or to represent altered states of consciousness as in a trance and dream. Modern dance may seem a long way from tribal dance but it isn't—it still uses fluid body movements to act out the expression of feelings and to represent order in a chaotic universe. Dance brings people closer together and allows close physical contact within a structured ritual (see page 15).

MOOD-ALTERING STATES

Dance alters our mood. It lifts us if we're feeling down. If we are feeling sad it can create instant euphoria. Different types of dance can generate different moods.

If you want to feel romantic, then try learning the waltz. If you want to feel sexy, then the samba or rhumba is for you. If you want to whoop with joy, try something energetic like an American square dance. If a more mellow feeling is what you seek, then a sedate, old-fashioned foxtrot or quickstep may be more suitable. There are rock and roll dances for the more daring amongst us: try the twist, jive, and shake. And if you want to go back to the elegance of the roaring Twenties, try the Charleston for great, silly fun.

JOINING A CLASS

Whatever form of dance you want to learn, now is the time to do it. Sign up for a class—you'd be surprised how many different dances you can learn. Don't be shy or nervous. The other members of your class will be used to beginners and will make you feel welcome. You'll love it. Once you've learned a few steps you'll be surprised how often you find yourself practicing— even when you're alone at home.

Commune with nature

Take a stroll in the countryside or along a beach. Walking is gentle and relaxing as long as we don't hurry or set our sights too high. Walking is not just a way of getting about but also a way of calming ourselves, reac-quainting ourselves with a more natural world. Combining walking with a nature hunt or beachcombing is fun and very therapeutic. It's like being a child again. Then we didn't hurry, we dawdled for hours looking at things. We walked and quite forgot where we were sup-posed to be going. We always had time to look at an interesting pebble, shell, or leaf.

TAKE A CHILD'S HAND

If you want to chill out and slow down, take the hand of a child and return to those golden days of unhurried walking along seashores or through woods. Or take the hand of the child within you and go back to the woods of your childhood. There's no need to tell you what to look for—it will find you. Among the fallen leaves and acorns there is a wealth of silence and relaxation. Kicking among driftwood and broken shells transports you into a world of calm and tranquillity.

ALLOW PLENTY OF TIME

Make sure you don't have anything planned, and leave your watch at home. Go somewhere you can walk in peace and just see what you find. While you are looking, something magic will happen. You'll also find more time than you ever thought possible.

Have a go at origami

Origami is a very relaxing therapy. A famous Argentine knife thrower—Ismael Adolfo Cerceda—used to practice the ancient art of paper folding before he went on stage to do his extremely dangerous act.

And origami has been promoted in schools to settle unruly children, used in mental hospitals to calm distressed patients, and even used to speed recovery from long illness. In 1914, Charles Gibbes was teaching paper folding to the nine-year-old son of the Russian Tsar when the boy began to speak English for the first time ever.

Origami is a helpful way to chill out because:

❖ *It can be practiced anywhere and at any time.*
❖ *Only a small amount of paper is needed.*
❖ *It's very good for hand/eye coordination.*
❖ *It's cheap.*
❖ *It starts off fairly simple and becomes as challenging as you want it to, giving great scope for improvement and experimentation.*
❖ *It's an amusing and entertaining skill that never fails to amuse and mystify.*

73

Make a wind chime

The melodic sound of a wind chime is very soothing. It's incredibly chilled to sit in the garden listening to light, natural music. Your wind chime will gently tinkle, jingle, and ring soothing notes of breeze-blown harmony. What could be more relaxing?

Wind-generated musical instruments are very old indeed. The idea originated in China at least 4,000 years ago—and the following designs are simple to make.

SIX-KEY WIND CHIME

You need six old keys, some clear nylon thread (fishing line is ideal), a small wooden hoop (one used for embroidery is fine), and some scissors.

Cut six equal lengths of thread about 18 inches long, and tie one key to each thread. Tie the other ends to the hoop at evenly spaced distances around its rim. Cut three lengths of thread about 12 inches long and tie each one to the hoop. Then tie the ends to each other in the center to form a loop—use this to hang your wind chime.

When the wind blows, your keys will gently tinkle in the breeze. It's quite fun to use keys that have become redundant—perhaps from your office—and so when the wind blows you are also being liberated from the locks of your past—and stressed—life.

FLOWERPOT WIND CHIME

You need one terracotta flowerpot, some narrow strips of metal, two small lengths of garden cane, lots of fishing twine, a pair of scissors, and a drill.

Turn the flowerpot upside down and place one of the sticks across the hole, which will now be at the top. Thread as many lengths of twine through the hole as you have pieces of metal. Drill a small hole in each piece of metal and take the twine through it. Tie the ends of the twine to the stick. Put the other stick on the underside of the hole and tie three one-foot lengths of twine to it. Pass these through the hole and tie the ends together to form a loop for hanging the wind chime. Once it is hung up, the pieces of metal will jingle against each

other and against the sides of the flow-erpot, creating a variety of melodic and unusual sounds.

METAL TUBE WIND CHIME

You need a flat, round piece of wood, seven lengths of copper tubing (get this from a hardware store), some fishing twine, and a drill.

Around the edge of the wooden circle drill ten small holes. Drill each copper tube at one end to make a hole to thread the twine through. Cut seven pieces of twine about 18 inches long. Thread one end through each tube and the other end through the holes you drilled in the wooden circle. Space these so that the three holes left over are at equal distances apart around the edge. Cut three lengths of twine about one foot in length and thread them through these "spare" holes. Tie the three lengths of twine together to make a hanging loop.

The copper tubes will jostle against each other in the wind, making a beautiful, haunting sound.

Print with potatoes

Simple printing with potatoes needn't be exclusively for children. You, too, can play! Remember that children make sure they have fun, whatever they're doing, and they don't mind making a mess. They love being creative. We can revitalize ourselves by doing likewise. Develop your own creative side by thinking of exciting designs to use and

HOW IT'S DONE

It's child's play! Find some large potatoes. Cut them in half and dry the cut ends on a paper towel. Carve your design with a sharp knife, or scoop it out with the end of a spoon. Make it as simple or as complex as you like. With a paintbrush, apply a little paint—water-based poster paint in vibrant colors

ways to use them. Make birthday cards, decorate a journal, or create friezes and wall decorations. Imagine decorating a whole room in wacky potato prints!

works best—and press down hard on your paper to leave a crisp-edged print. If you want to be really creative, try using different colors on one potato!

Write a short story

Keep your creativity by using it. Short story writing is a very personal way of keeping the intellectual juices flowing. This is a private fantasy world for you alone to enjoy. Your characters act and think in the way that you want them to. Life conforms to your rules. Just put pen to paper and get writing!

Here are some titles and first sentences to help you get started.

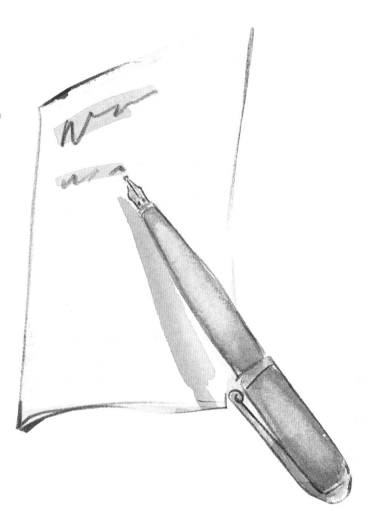

TITLES:

❖ *"The Dead Mole"*
❖ *"Mrs. Stubbins' Shock"*
❖ *"We Found an Artifact"*

FIRST SENTENCES:

❖ *The day the balloon landed we were all...*
❖ *All the color was missing, and we knew that it had...*
❖ *There was nothing for it, Agatha had to open the door, but her heart was beating so fast...*
❖ *Jack wanted the farm so badly that he thought of nothing else, talked of nothing else, and now it was for sale...*

Give yourself a massage

Being pampered is a fantastic way to chill out. It makes us feel loved, accepted, appreciated, and cared for. Sometimes we simply need a bit of pampering. Self-massage is a great way to pamper yourself. It relieves stress, helps you to relax, eases tension—headaches and muscular aches and pains—and enhances well-being.

Massage used to be much more a natural part of our lives. It soothes crying babies—a use that's gradually coming back into fashion—eases painful limbs, and acts as a general comforter. Many ailments suffered in today's world are directly attributable to stress. Muscles get locked with tension and repressed fear and anger. The kneading and stroking movements of massage can release these tensions.

Self-massage—like all massage—is beneficial in two important areas:

Physical
❖ *Relaxes and loosens tight or strained muscles*
❖ *Stimulates oxygen flow*

Mental
❖ *Eliminates stress and tension*
❖ *Increases focus and concentration*

SCALP MASSAGE
One of the best ways to relieve head tension is to get the blood circulating between the skin, skull, and brain. A scalp massage is guaranteed to get the blood moving.

Place your hands on your scalp, right at the roots of your hair. Spread your fingers and thumbs out to cover as much of your scalp as possible. Starting at the nape of your neck and mov-

MASSAGING YOUR TEMPLES

Bring your elbows down to your desk and place your hands on your temples. Using small circular motions, gently rub the skin clockwise and then counter-clockwise. Do this for ten long breaths.

BACK MASSAGE

Wooden back massages (pictured left) can be blissful to use. If you haven't got one, here's an alternative. Sitting upright in your chair, place a tennis ball in the small of your back and lean back in the chair. Press against the ball and breathe deeply. Take about ten breaths. Relax and repeat if you need to.

ing forward, gently rotate the hair roots in little clockwise motions. Make sure you are breathing long and deeply to promote oxygen flow to the tight areas of the scalp. Take ten deep breaths, massaging as you breathe. Next, change direction: massage counterclockwise, starting at the forehead and moving backward.

HEAD MASSAGE

Rest one elbow on a desk, hand and forearm parallel to your spine. Lift the heel of one hand to the space between your eyebrows. Allow all the weight of your head to fall onto the heel of your hand. Breathe deeply.

Make small clockwise rotations with the heel of your hand. Repeat using counterclockwise movements.

Press some flowers

Pressing flowers is absorbing and rewarding. It distracts you from work and worries, and takes you outside to pick flowers in the fresh air.

Press flowers from your own garden or common flowers from the wild. You can press a flower to commemorate a marriage or a birth. Having a memento of a special occasion is very reassuring—some of the color and magic of the day remains seemingly forever.

WHAT YOU NEED

You can buy a flower press from a craft store but the simplest flower press is made from the pages of a heavy book. Open the book at a place roughly in the middle and place a piece of blotting paper inside. Arrange your flowers on this and then place another piece of blotting paper on top. Shut the book and place several other large books on top to weight it down. Leave the book like this for a month or two and you will have a perfectly pressed reminder of a special day.

Visualize creatively

We live in a world of computers, metal, plastic, and instant everything. But our responses are firmly rooted in a much earlier age. The more we pretend to have it all under control, the more stressed we are and the less in touch with our true selves we become. By using creative imagery and visualization, we can put ourselves back in touch with a more natural world—one in which we actually belong and can feel at peace.

Children have a natural ability to visualize creatively. They run about in the woods and see the trees as living entities, walk in the meadows and chat to imaginary friends and spirits, romp in their bedrooms and people them with imaginary creatures from mythology and folklore.

As adults we have to learn to let go and lose ourselves in child-like dreams once more, to let go of the pretensions and inhibitions that come with being adults and somehow apart from the world of the imagination.

Next time you go out of the house, half-close your eyes and see if you can see your surroundings through a child's eyes—the mystery of it all, the wonder, the colors, the excitement of discovering a world that's new and fresh. Try to visualize the wild essence of nature, peopled with spirits and beings of light. Use your imagination. Be creative. Visualize a world where nature's lore still holds sway.

When you need to relax, find a comfortable place where you won't be disturbed and close your eyes. Visualize a place where you have been very happy—a beach from a vacation or a secret part of the countryside. Capture the essence of the place again as you conjure it up in your mind. Feel the air on your cheek, hear the sounds in your inner ear, and re-create the smells in your mind. As you lose yourself in your visualization you'll relax and relive the moment.

Hang out in a hammock

In this book we cover many chill-out techniques. But there is one that simply tops them all—relaxing in a hammock. This is the epitome of indulgent bliss, of lazy, languid afternoons with nothing to do except read a little and sleep a lot. Lazing in a hammock brings instant relief from the cares of this world. Try it—it really works! It has also been said that time spent cocooned in a hammock adds to your lifespan, so spend as much time as you can hanging around in one!

CONSTRUCTION

If you are lucky enough to have two trees, spaced a suitable distance apart, in your backyard, plus unlimited amounts of sunshine, you're halfway there. If not, don't stress yourself out trying to construct a frame for your hammock—the most chilled method is to get someone else to do the hard work! If you only have one tree, a wooden A-frame can be constructed from which to hang the other end of the hammock. If you don't have any trees, some hammocks come with readymade metal frames to hang them in. If you want an indoor hammock, get a professional to hang up some big hooks.

HAMMOCK ETIQUETTE

If you keep falling out of your hammock, you probably need a bigger one. Many hammocks are too narrow to be truly comfortable. Buy one made for two and you'll find it is just the right size.

Getting out is easy. Swing your legs over the side. Let your feet touch the ground and walk backward until you can stand up. Simple!

Do Chinese exercises

Ancient Chinese exercises are perfect for rejuvenating, refreshing, and revitalizing yourself. They are holistic—that is they exercise the body, the mind, and the emotions—and are, therefore, a good way to stay healthy and live a long life. They help us maintain equilibrium, and can speed recovery from illness and surgery. They also help to relieve tension and keep us supple, which is great for an all-round feeling of relaxation.

These exercises are drawn from disciplines such as Tai Chi, Chi Kung, and Yi Jin Ying—all systems for exercising the body as well as healing therapies.

Guidelines

❖ *Practice all movements gently and softly. Breathe smoothly and naturally.*
❖ *Take your time and enjoy the exercises—there is no need to rush.*
❖ *Relax your body at all times and don't tense anything—do the exercises as effortlessly as you can.*
❖ *Focus on what you're doing.*
❖ *Don't exercise if you feel tired or ill, or after a meal.*

EXERCISES FOR VITALITY

EXERCISE 1 Stand with your feet shoulder-width apart. Take a step to the right and bend your elbows, putting your fingertips on your shoulders. Stretch out your arms to the side, level with your shoulders. Keep your elbows straight and your palms turned up. Bring your arms back to the starting position of fingers on the shoulders and step back. Take a step to the left and repeat the exercise. Repeat the whole exercise ten times.

EXERCISE 2 Do as you did for exercise 1, but this time instead of bringing your fingertips back to your shoulders, bring them together so the fingers of both hands meet just under your chin, palms down. Then bring your arms back out again, palms up, and finally back to resting on your shoulders. Repeat the whole exercise ten times.

EXERCISE 3 Stand with your feet fairly wide apart and your hands on your hips. Bend at the waist to the right and

Chinese exercises

stretch your right arm back and up, with the palm turned up, until it is level with your shoulder. Bend back and return your hand to your hip. Keep your other hand on your other hip at all times. Repeat the exercise with your left arm. Do the whole exercise ten times on each side.

FITNESS EXERCISES

EXERCISE 1 Stand with your feet shoulder-width apart. Place your hands on your hips. Move your pelvis clockwise in a circular motion for about a minute. Then switch and move counterclockwise for the same length of time. Be relaxed and enjoy the movement. You can sway as much as you like and, as you get fitter, do it for longer.

EXERCISE 2 Stand with your feet slightly wider apart than your shoulders. Put your arms at your sides and bring your hands up until your palms are facing forward, elbows bent, forearms against the side of your body—as if you were about to push on a wall very close

to you. Bend your knees so you are half squatting and, at the same time, push your hands forward slowly. You can put a lot of effort into this if you want—it helps strengthen all your muscles, but especially the ones in your legs. Return to the starting position and repeat the whole exercise ten times.

EXERCISE 3 Stand with your feet together. Lift your right foot, bring it back behind your body and then sharply kick forward. Bring the foot back and repeat with the other foot. Continue doing this exercise, alternating with your left and right feet ten times with each foot. After some practice, you will establish a nice fluid motion and build a relaxing rhythm.

EXERCISES FOR WELL-BEING

EXERCISE 1 Stand with your feet slightly wider apart than your shoulders. Bring both arms up above your head, fingers extended as far as they will go and breathe in deeply. Squat down and let your arms fall back to your sides,

...continued

then breathe out slowly. Rise up and again lift your arms above your head while breathing in deeply. Squat again, let your arms fall, and breathe out. Repeat this exercise ten times.

EXERCISE 2 Lie on your back on the floor with your arms by your side. Bring your knees up until you are in the fetal position but still on your back. Roll over onto your right side. Roll back onto your back and roll to the other side, then back onto your back again. Repeat the exercise ten times.

EXERCISE 3. Lie on your back, arms by your sides. Bring your knees up until you can put your feet flat on the floor. Bring your arms up above your head. Move your arms back to your sides and your legs flat again. Repeat ten times.

RELAXATION EXERCISES

Finish your session with these exercises, which can help to lower blood pressure, reduce the incidence of headaches, and increase general well-being.

EXERCISE 1 Stand with your feet shoulder-width apart. Swing your arms backward and forward—one moving forward while the other is going backward—and at the same time, gently swing your lower back and pelvis backward and forward as well. Do this for three or four minutes whenever you feel tense or tired.

EXERCISE 2 Stand with your feet together and your arms by your sides. Take a step forward with your right foot and stretch both arms upward. Bring your arms back down and step back. Repeat with the other foot. Repeat the whole thing ten times, each time bringing your feet back together.

EXERCISE 3 Stand with your feet shoulder-width apart and your hands on your hips. Twist to the left and bring your left arm up with the palm up. Slowly lower your arm until your hand is again on your hip, twisting back to the front as you do so. Repeat the exercise ten times with each arm.

Get juggling

Learning to juggle requires intense concentration but virtually no conscious thought. While you focus on the balls, something happens to the space in your head. All those niggling worries disappear, and you end your session feeling calm and tranquil.

WHAT DO I NEED?

Find a set of three juggling balls. Start with beanbag juggling balls—which don't bounce—and face an armchair. That way when you drop a ball you don't have to bend so far to pick it up.

HOW TO JUGGLE

Begin by lightly tossing one ball between your hands in an arc shape. When you feel confident with that, try tossing two balls from hand to hand in an arc so that the balls cross over in midair but don't touch. When you've mastered that, throw the two balls alternatively so your pattern is throw, throw, catch, catch. And when you're happy doing that, take two balls in one hand and one in the other and juggle—throw, throw, catch, throw, catch, catch. Honestly—it really is that easy!

Rewrite your life story

Making judgements about whether we've failed at something in the past makes us sad and apprehensive. But you can change all that by rewriting your life story and reinventing yourself.

Imagine that at the age of twelve you ran away to join the circus or you became a film stunt person instead of what you've turned out to be. How would you see yourself? Imagine you're a novelist and your publisher wants a short biography for the cover. What are you going to write? If you had an unhappy childhood, did badly in your exams, flunked high school, and got fired from your first job, would you say all that? Much better to say you had an idyllic childhood, passed every exam with flying colors, graduated with honors, started your first job and were made president of the company within a year because you were so smart.

Write that biography now. Have fun and let your imagination know no bounds. This is a fun chill-out technique designed to raise your spirits and change the past.

Light up your life

Candles evoke a mood of romance, relaxation, spirituality, and calm. They come in many shapes and colors. Making your own candles is fun. Don't worry if they don't come out quite as you expected. Just so long as you chill out and enjoy.

WHAT YOU NEED

An old can

An old saucepan that you can devote to candle making

Molds—from a craft store

Wicks

A long wooden spoon to stir the melted wax

Three-inch sticky tape

One-inch sticky tape

Scissors

Wax

Scents and dyes, optional

How to make molded candles

❖ *Lightly coat the mold with oil.*
❖ *Prepare the wick—this should just be question of threading the wick through the mold, but follow the* manufacturer's instructions.
❖ *Slowly melt the wax in a pot placed over a saucepan of boiling water.*
❖ *Add any dyes and/or scents you want to use.*
❖ *Pour the melted wax into the mold.*
❖ *Let it set for at least eight hours.*

❖ *Top off the mold after the wax has settled and leave it to harden.*
❖ *Remove the candle from the mold and trim the wick. Now you can burn it!*

If you want to make your own molds, you can use any heatproof container.

Try using a flowerpot. Make sure the hole in the bottom is plugged and put a pencil across the top to support the wick. Oil the container and fill with molten wax. Light your flowerpot candle and it will burn for many hours, giving off a mysterious and relaxing light.

Meditate with a mandala

A mandala is a ancient eastern aid to meditation, in the form of a circular, geometric pattern. Make your own with compasses and coloring pens or paints.

With the compasses, draw a large circle on a piece of card stock. Using narrow lines, divide it into equal segments through the center of the circle.

Within the circle draw another five circles, each getting smaller towards the center—and each the same distance apart. You now have a series of circles focused on the center by straight lines. Fill each tiny section with a different color, or for a striking effect, fill alternative sections in just two colors.

Instead of circles, you could use a series of diminishing squares or triangles. Keep to regular shapes, as irregular ones lead the eye away from the center.

USING YOUR MANDALA

Once you have drawn your mandala—creating it is just as relaxing as using it—you are ready to meditate. Prop the mandala up in front of you and focus on the very center of it. Keep it in the forefront of your mind. Each time your eyes—or your thoughts—begin to wander, bring them back to the center. Relax and concentrate, and eventually the central point of the mandala will slowly begin to form a cloud of blue light. Focus on this light and enjoy the feeling of relaxation and tranquillity it brings.

Get knotted

What is it about a piece of rope that simply calls out for a knot? Like wood whittling (see page 65), it is one of those occupations that can be both gloriously aimless and satisfying. You can while away many happy hours with just a piece of rope and your imagination, with busy hands and an empty brain. It is also great fun to learn some of the more complicated knots—sheep shanks and bowlines, clove hitches and flag bends. You can get a deep sense of satisfaction from mastering the techniques and making sense of the complex diagrams you will find in a knotting book. And once you've learned the basics, you'll be a useful person to have around, especially if you're keen on boating!

KNOTTING WITH STRING

Aimlessly tying knots in rope is one thing, but if you want to create something beautiful and useful, too, try the ancient art of macramé. This craft, named after an Arabic word for knotted fringe, saw a resurgence in the 1960s, when it was used to make decorative items for the home such as plant holders and wall hangings. Maybe it's time for a revival in the name of all things chilled!

Fill a vase with fresh flowers

If your home is adorned with the heavenly scent of freshly cut flowers, you will automatically feel relaxed, soothed, and in touch with nature. Flowers are beautiful however they are arranged, but it's worth learning how to place them like the professionals.

The most important point is to keep it simple. The key words are color, scale, proportion, and balance. The simplest way to arrange flowers is in a vase.

WHAT TO USE

It's great fun to use flowers from your garden. If you're lucky enough to have them in season, try hyacinths, delphiniums, lilies, cherry blossom, golden rod, narcissus, orchids, long-stemmed roses, tulips, or daffodils. Cut the stems with pruning shears. Or you can buy flowers from a florist, even when they are out of season. If you're short on flowers, use fresh, green foliage to fill out your arrangement—it will complement the colors and some of it smells deliciously earthy. You can also use grasses, twigs, mosses, fir cones, or even vegetables. Instead of vases, try pots, urns, baskets, trays, bowls, buckets, old watering cans, or jam jars.

Try this simple flower arrangement.

WHAT YOU NEED

A large, shallow bowl

Two blocks of florist's "oasis"

Adhesive tape, wire, and scissors

A large bunch of flowers from your garden, plus some moss

Soak the "oasis" blocks in water and anchor them into the bowl with adhesive tape. Arrange the flowers with the tallest stems in the center of the blocks, and the smaller stems in a spiral around the tallest ones, with the very shortest nearest the bowl's edge. Leave a gap between the flowers and the edge of the bowl and fill it with moss—attach this with short pieces of wire.

Absorb yourself in a jigsaw

There's something almost akin to meditation about doing a jigsaw. It's so all-consuming that, while you're concentrating on finding the pieces, your mind simply can't focus on anything else. Something mysteriously and wonderfully relaxing happens, and you will find you are completely chilled out without even having to try!

To begin with, tackle a fairly simple jigsaw that has no more than a hundred pieces. These can usually be completed in a satisfyingly short length of time. Make sure that it has a picture that you like—this is vital if you want your mind really to become engaged. Then try moving on to a more challenging jigsaw, of five hundred pieces or more. If you get stuck, don't get frustrated—leave the jigsaw where it is. When you can come back to it, more pieces will magically fit into place.

Make some noise!

To chill out you need to relax. To relax you need to de-stress. To de-stress you need to get rid of pent-up anger, frustration, resentment, and disappointment. There's no better therapy than banging a drum. It's an instant release. By beating out a rhythm you beat out all that anger, drive out the demons of despair, and are filled with tranquillity.

New Age stores stock basic ethnic drums. Or you could buy a folk drum and stick from a music store. But for serious stress relief, beat a waist-height African drum so you can stand up and give it all you've got. Try it—you'll feel much better for it!

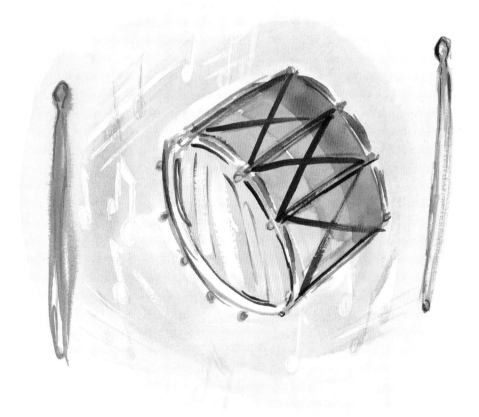

Tie-dye with natural dyes

Tie-dyeing is creative, experimental, good exercise (when you get out and about to collect the natural dyes), and—most of all—fun. It's a way of jazzing up an article of clothing by tying it in a knot, or tying it up very tightly with string, and dyeing it. When the dye "takes" it leaves gaps that are partially dyed, creating weird and wonderful patterns and colorful abstract swirls.

HOW IT'S DONE

Experiment with something old to begin with. White fabrics take dye very well. To tie-dye a pair of trousers, tie each leg every six inches for stripes. Or tie the legs together very tightly to get random patterns. Or wrap the whole pair of trousers into a ball tied with string. The darker dye will take more darkly on the outside, and it will gradually get lighter as it works its way into the center.

NATURAL DYE

Ever eaten blackberries and gotten stained fingers? They stain a wonderful, dark red. Try using other soft fruits—raspberries, blackcurrants, loganberries, and blueberries. Experiment with plants and leaves—onion skins for brown, beets for purple, saffron for yellow, and agrimony for gray.

WHAT YOU NEED

A large bowl that can withstand very hot water and won't stain

A wooden spoon for stirring—choose one you don't mind getting stained

Clothes to be dyed

2 pounds blackberries or other natural dye

1 pound salt to "fix" the dye

These quantities of blackberries and salt will dye one or maybe two garments.

Boil up the blackberries in a saucepan with hot water and the salt. Tie up your garment. Put it into the bowl and pour the hot blackberry, salt, and water mixture over it. Give the whole thing a good stir. The longer you leave it the darker the color will be, and the more likely it is that the dye will seep through and dye the entire gar-

ment. Take it out after ten minutes. Drain and leave to dry. This should take about two hours, but you can speed up the process by putting the garment into a clothes drier—still tied up. Don't undo it until it's thoroughly dry. Then you should have a magnificent, beautifully patterned, blackberry-colored garment.

Get in touch

We all lose touch with old friends and members of our family. People move away, and we promise to stay in touch, promise to write, promise not to forget them. But then life gets in the way and suddenly it's five years since we last spoke to them. The underlying guilt can cause stress; it's better to keep those promises.

Tracking someone down after a long time can be difficult. If you do have problems, try the Internet. Nowadays many people have an email address and there are plenty of search engines that will trace people quickly and for free. Imagine how surprised your friend will be to get your email.

I know someone who recently traced an old friend he hadn't seen for over 50 years. The friend was delighted. A tearful reunion took place, which re-established a valuable friendship that might otherwise have been lost forever. Children and grandchildren met who might otherwise never have done so, and they became friends as well. A whole new network of friendships was established by sending a single email.

Explore your environment

If you want to chill out and live a long and happy life, you need to feel you belong. People who have a fully developed sense of belonging rarely suffer stress-related illnesses. If you want to belong to your local community you need to know and explore it, understand it, and incorporate it into your own worldview.

Urban exploration is a wonderful way of finding out how your community came into being, what happens in every quarter of it, who lives where, who designed and built your town, its history and culture, its potential future, and its impact on the environment.

GO FOR A WALK

Your first step is to do some exploring on foot. I mean real exploring, not just strolling around the area. Set yourself the task of covering every street within a mile's vicinity of your home—there are always plenty of new sights to discover just on your doorstep.

ASK QUESTIONS

As you go, ask yourself questions. Consider why that street has an unusual name, what happens in that community hall around the corner, why the architecture changes from street to street. Make a mental list of questions you need answers to in order to gain a full picture of your community.

GET THE FACTS

Next, hit the books. Go to your local library or museum. See if there is an archive section that contains local information. Study detailed maps of the area and identify all the local landmarks. Try to find maps from a hundred years ago so you can see how it has changed. It is often useful to look at old census returns—you might come across some of your own ancestors. This quest for information can become an on-going project. And you can relax in the knowledge that you know everything there is to know about your town!

Paint a watercolor

People who fly into a rage easily are three times more likely than the rest of us to have a heart attack. They are the classic go-getters—competitive and aggressive. They think predominantly with the right side of the brain, the side that deals with logic, problem-solving, and non-emotional thought processes.

It's just as important—if not more so—to exercise the left side of the brain, which deals with artistic expression, intuition, and emotions. Psychologists recommend taking up a hobby purely for relaxation and not as a competitive activity. Watercolor painting is ideal because it takes a long time to get good at it. You paint purely for pleasure and learn something about your artistic creative side along the way.

You don't need to buy expensive paints. All you need is a child's paintbox, a pad of presoaked watercolor paper, a brush or two, and a jar of water.

Find a quiet place. Before you begin anything, hold the paints and allow them to speak to you. You are merely the conduit for their artistic expression.

Take a brush and dip it into the water. Wet a little of the page and see what effect you get. Take up a little of one color from your box, and gently place it on the wet page. See what it does. Allow the color to run and mix freely with the water. You aren't painting a scene—just learning what color, water, and paper say to each other, how they combine to create an effect.

Use only one color at first. Play with it. Create broad strokes, drop color onto the paper. Experiment with a different color until you have used each color once. Then try combining two colors.

You can play with color and water for months before you even attempt to paint a scene that could be called representational. Enjoy this process of discovery and relish the calm it brings.

Keep a reading journal

We all enjoy the escapism of reading a really good book. And keeping a reading journal is a useful and chilled way to keep track of our reading. It's good to be able to remind ourselves of the pleasure we took in each book we have read, and it helps us to decide which books to reread.

WHAT YOU NEED

This is easy. All you need is a notebook. Jot down what you read, who wrote it, when you read it, why, and what you thought of it. It's a simple record of books that brought you pleasure.

WE CHANGE

Our moods change. Sometimes we read a book because we feel down or are looking for an answer, and a particular book might satisfy our needs at the time. Later, when we are feeling more positive, we might reread it and get something completely different from it. Keeping a reading journal is a useful way of charting our progress, to see how far we have come.

Make a mosaic

Making a mosaic can be creative and absorbing, relaxing and fun.

Before you break any china, practice with paper first—use wallpaper, gift wrapping paper, or plain paper in different colors. Play with shapes and colors, enjoying the pleasing juxtapositions of each. Design a simple pattern with your pieces.

At this stage, decide where you would like to put your mosaic. On a wall? On an old garden table that needs a new lease of life? It helps to design your mosaic in paper before you make it up for real.

HAVE A SMASHING TIME

Now it's time to let out all your pent-up aggression. Buy up lots of old china plates and saucers from charity stores, put them into a well-padded bag (a large, clean vacuum cleaner bag is ideal for this), and smash them to smithereens. Wear garden gloves to protect yourself from the jagged edges.

Refer back to the design you did earlier and lay out your pieces on a flat surface. Once you have a pattern you're happy with, start gluing. Lift a piece at a time and apply glue to the back.

Once all the pieces are glued in place

they need grouting—apply the grout to the gaps between the pieces.

There's no need to stop at china. Add pebbles, glass, wood, metal, brick, or even shells. There are no limits!

Write a love poem

This is one for the softies, the romantics, the lovers, the dreamers.

Forget everything you learned in school about poetry. There are no rules. A poem is a collection of words—no more and no less. How you choose to arrange the words is up to you.

WHAT'S A LOVE POEM?

A love poem expresses your love for someone, some thing, some energy, some force—whatever you choose. You choose what you want to express and to whom or what. It might be a prayer to your own personal god or a declaration of undying devotion to your partner —or intended partner.

WHAT IS LOVE?

If we knew the answer we'd be very wise. But we don't. No one knows what love is. It's an indescribable force of nature, a coming together of two things that need to be together, no matter what.

HOW TO START

Get some paper, a pencil, and an eraser. Ink is too permanent. With a pencil you can erase, overwrite, cross out, and generally feel much more like a love poet.

Sit in a quiet space, close your eyes, and imagine who or what you love is in front of you. Describe in a few words how you feel. Use word pictures to summon up your feelings. How about the following?

❖ *I feel like fresh snow when I see your face.*

❖ *You make me feel like I'm at the first sunset in the world when we kiss.*

❖ *Your nearness is as if all the fireworks in all the world had just gone off.*

The rest is up to you.

Go fly a kite

If you really want to lighten your mood and have fun, then go fly a kite. Imagine being out on a windy hill in the spring air with nothing to do but enjoy yourself. Kite flying is very therapeutic and relaxing. There is something symbolic about a kite—as it rises into the air, your mood lifts. And when the wind drops and your kite crashes to the ground, you can visualize it as all your worries crashing into the earth to be absorbed and dissipated. And, of course, for sheer exhilaration, nothing beats flying a kite on a windy day. It gets you out in the open, fills your lungs with fresh air, and puts the roses back in your cheeks.

WHAT SORT OF KITE?

You can buy a kite very cheaply from a toy store. Old-fashioned box kites are still the best to start off with. Or it's quite easy to make your own.

Once you've got the hang of how to control your simple kite, you can move onto lozenge-shaped ones and stunt kites. When you are at a more advanced stage of kite-flying skill, the complexity and daring of kite fighting can be ultraexhilarating!

Do some modeling

Model making is rewarding and fun. When you were a child, poring over a model kit, a tube of glue, and some enamel paints probably kept you quiet and out of trouble for hours. Things are no different when you're an adult—adults need to have fun and be creative, too. Having an absorbing hobby reduces stress. And, of course, you get something to show for it when you've finished all the hard work.

MODEL KITS

A good introduction to the wide world of model making is to go down to the toy store and get yourself a model kit. There is a vast range of these available, some very easy, others absorbingly complicated. Choose an easy one first, which won't take long to put together and will help you to build up the skills to tackle more difficult ones. You can buy kits that depict many different things: planes, trains, automobiles, boats, farm machinery, buildings, and even people.

The golden rule of putting together a successful model kit is to take your time.

There are so many delicate operations involved in assembling the tiny pieces that the process simply won't work if you rush your way through the kit—and you certainly won't be satisfied if your end result looks unfinished or slapdash.

TAKING IT FURTHER

Once you've completed a kit or two, you might feel confident enough to move onto making your own models. Model making is the kind of hobby that can take over your whole life—this could be your chance to construct that replica of the Statue of Liberty out of matchsticks!

Models can be made of any material you like—wood, metal, paper, plastic, or household junk can be commandeered to make models depicting anything your imagination wants them to. Try making a model of your own house, garden, or street. Or you could be even more ambitious and attempt a model of your whole town, at any scale and in as little or as much detail as you wish. The possibilities are truly endless!

Get rid of clutter

The basic principle of feng shui is that energy—chi—flows through harmonious buildings, bringing health and vitality. If forced through cluttered buildings that trap the energy or impede the flow, then it stagnates and becomes sha—noxious vapors, which bring ill health, depression, listlessness, and apathy. If you're feeling lethargic and out of sorts, it might be your home that's at fault.

Make space to think and breathe. Surrounded by clutter, you're unable to spread your wings. A downward spiral of apathy breeds disinterest, so you feel unable to clear the space.

THE KITCHEN

Open the cupboards and take a deep breath. Throw out everything that's past its expiration date, old, battered, unused in the past six months, rusty, broken, chipped, or dusty. This includes pots and pans, utensils, food, plates, cups, and containers. You're aiming for a completely empty space to start again in. Be ruthless.

THE SITTING ROOM

William Morris once said that you should never have anything in your home you do not know to be useful or believe to be beautiful. Make that your mission statement. Look at ornaments. Beautiful? Useful? If they are neither, throw them away. Clear out magazines, newspapers, cupboards, and under sofas and chairs. Clean out the fireplace and fill it with fresh flowers if you don't use it. Empty wastepaper baskets. Vacuum the curtains. Think about redecorating.

THE BEDROOM

Throw open the wardrobe door. Throw out anything that doesn't fit you, is old and tired, is torn or worn, doesn't suit you (be honest), is out of fashion, you haven't worn in the past six months, is cheap, tacky, garish, tasteless, or is made of synthetic materials. Now go under the bed—clear everything. Clear out bedside tables, alcoves, and dressing tables. Clear space like your life depends on it.

THE BATHROOM

Chuck out anything old or worn out such as toothbrushes and razors. Empty cupboards, clean around the tub, clear countertops and shelves. Put away everything that isn't being used that you want to keep.

Do this for every room in your house. When you've finished you'll have at least ten full black plastic bags. Don't delay—throw them all away or take them to your local charity store.

Then look around your home and enjoy the freedom of space, space, space.

Make a pilgrimage

Making a pilgrimage adds an extra dimension to life. It makes us focus on our spirituality in a very real and practical way. We all need to take time out to think about where we're going in our lives. Making a pilgrimage gives us time to think about real, deep, and serious things in a place of tranquillity.

CHOOSING A DESTINATION

Visit a religious building: a church, mosque, synagogue, or temple. Find a place connected with someone you admire—Emily Dickinson's house or Graceland. Or find a suitable landmark—a very old and venerated tree, a deep and mysterious lake, or the top of a mountain. Pick something that can be achieved in a weekend. Plan to walk the first day and stay the night at a small hostel, and then finish your walk on the following day so that you arrive suitably tired, but not exhausted, on the evening of the second day. Arrange to have a friend pick you up.

As you walk, focus on the really important things about yourself, not what you do at work or home but how you will answer for your actions and what karma you're storing up for yourself. As you walk, concentrate on where you're going and why. If you practice an organized religion, there will be prayers to say or chants to perform. But if you follow a more natural view, sing as you go, talk to your own gods, make peace with your heart, purge yourself of doubt, guilt, and fear.

Compose a haiku

Today, crosswords and other word games are the relaxation technique of choice for millions of people across the world. It seems that wrapping one's brain around the intricacies of language can be extremely therapeutic. Here's another way to use words to clear your brain of unwanted stress.

A haiku is a traditional and ancient Japanese poem. It's made up of three lines that are arranged in a limited number of syllables. The first line contains five syllables, the second line seven, and the third line five again. Notice that we're talking syllables here, not words.

In the Japanese tradition, the first two lines paint a picture or set a scene, then the third line adds a comment, makes an observation, or makes a point about why the scene has been set and what we are to learn from it.

Haikus were used as an aid to meditation. The third line was a sort of Zen revelation or a step towards enlightenment. Nowadays the third line is often humorous. It surprises or fills in a detail that was missing, sometimes utterly changing our mental visualization of the haiku's first two lines.

Japanese haikus translated into English will not, unless very skillfully done, read as five-seven-five. But like this one, they're still fascinating:

Snow melts,
and the village overflows—
with children.

Making up your own haiku is great fun and very therapeutic. You can treat it as much as a word game as a poem. Composing a haiku encourages you to use just the right words:

I study haiku
At the feet of the master
Very bad posture

Simply choose your subject, meditate upon it for a while, and then put pen to paper. Sometimes the words come out immediately, but often you can find yourself spending hour after absorbing hour honing the words to perfection.

Reduce your stress level with reflexology

Reflexology is an ancient diagnostic technique from China and India in which the soles of the feet are massaged deeply. It uses the feet to prevent and soothe disease in the rest of the body. It works on similar principles to acupuncture. Meridians—energy lines—travel throughout the body carrying life-giving energy. These meridians end in the soles of the feet, so massaging the correct area of the feet frees up the energy and allows it to flow again to the affected part of the body. There is not enough space in this book to explore the ins and outs of medical reflexology; however, simple reflexology and foot massage can be marvellous for relieving stress and reducing tension.

EXPLORE YOUR FEET

Gently feel all over your feet until you feel areas of tenderness or what feels like "grit" under the surface of the skin. These are the key areas to massage. Apply pressure with the edge of your thumb and rotate your thumb clockwise. Push quite hard—or as hard as you can stand. Do this for as long as you like—the longer you go on, the more relaxed you'll feel.

Reflexology is good for relieving stress and tension, helping you to sleep, soothing away any fears and worries, and generally toning your system. Although you can feel the benefits when you massage your own feet, it's even better when somebody else does it for you!

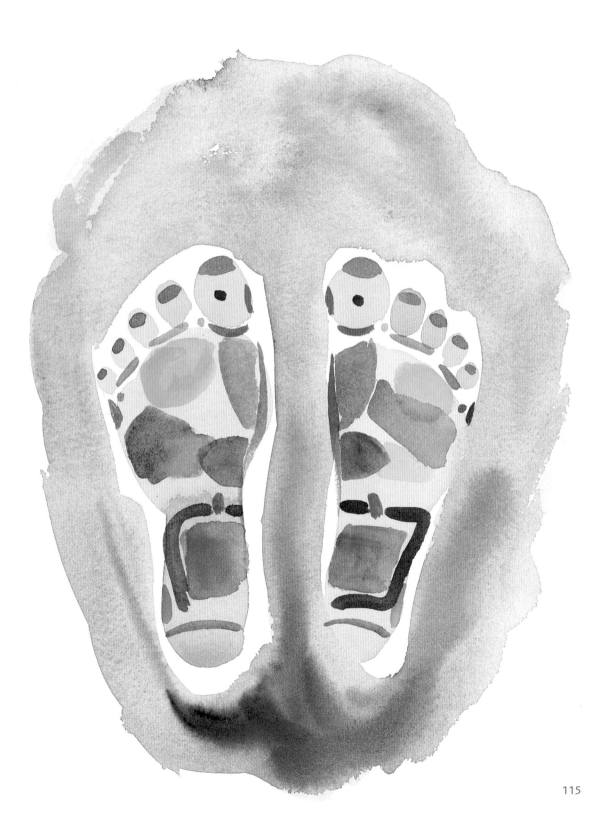

chill out

Write a journal

Keeping a journal is not the same as keeping a diary. A diary records events as they happen—usually on a daily basis. A journal is a record of impressions, feelings, emotions, and responses over a much longer period of time. It doesn't have to be completed each day. It can be updated once a week or even once a month. In it you record what has happened to you during that time—not as events but as experience. This way over the years you see patterns, notice changes and progress, and monitor your growth.

A BETTER HUMAN BEING

A journal records how you change into a better adult, a nicer person, a more relaxed human being. A journal is a useful way of looking back and seeing how far you have come.

In your journal you can record:

❖ *How things happened*
❖ *Why they happened*
❖ *What you felt when they happened*
❖ *What your response was*
❖ *How you felt afterwards*
❖ *What steps you took to recover the situation or celebrate it*
❖ *How you feel about such events happening again*

HAPPY?

Someone once said that happy people don't keep journals. This isn't necessarily true. A journal is a very private way of counseling yourself and can help you to overcome sadness or consolidate happiness. It can be helpful to add notes in the margin when you look back and see what happened and how you might have responded better to a situation.

POUR YOUR HEART OUT

If you're going through a bad time, a journal gives you a chance to pour your heart out, to get all your feelings out, to purge negative emotions, to express anger and disappointment, to cry, to allow yourself to hurt, to record your sorrow and pain, and most importantly, to make sense of the world. A journal is a confessor. It merely listens as you write. Once you bounce back you might not write as often. And that's the beauty of a journal—you can write whenever you feel like it. There's no pressure, no timetable, and no deadline.

A journal kept over many years is a record of all your hopes and fears, your dreams and successes, your failures and disappointments. It is a perfect time capsule of your life.

Bring back the zing

Feeling sluggish? No energy? A vitality drink made from a blend of fruits and vegetables can restore the balance in your diet, replace lost vitamins and minerals, increase energy levels, and truly bring back the zing into your life.

You will need a blender and a basket full of your favorite fruits and vegetables. Spend an afternoon blending.

Use your favorite organic fruit and vegetables, the freshest you can get. Add plain yogurt for texture or more fruit juice to dilute it. Make it fresh and natural, with no sugar.

Autumn fruits such as blackberries, plums, grapes, and pears blend together well. A useful rule is that any fruits that grow at the same time of year blend well and any fruits that grow in the same climatic conditions blend well.

VEGETABLES

Vegetables that are easy to blend include tomatoes, carrots, and peppers. A good rule is to use only vegetables that you would eat raw anyway. Potatoes will never make a tasty juice drink!

FRUIT

It's time to experiment. Try blending bananas, apples, plain yogurt, and almonds. Try leaving out the yogurt and adding apple juice. A mixture of milk, bananas, almonds, natural plain chocolate, sunflower seeds, chopped apple, and a spoonful of honey is great for getting you going in the mornings.

FRUIT AND VEGETABLES

Fruit and vegetables blended together can result in some intriguing flavors. Try carrot, apple, and walnut with natural apple juice. Or tomato, carrot, apple, and a little Tabasco. Avoid blending citrus fruits with winter vegetables—they don't do anything for each other. Keep experimenting!

Listen to music

Music soothes the savage beast. Make music therapy your soothing key to relaxation. Music has been used for healing for centuries in virtually every culture. It brings people together for relaxation and to evoke moods and responses. It's also a powerful way of expressing feelings nonverbally. Music is a safe way to express feelings that might otherwise remain bottled up.

There are three types of music therapy—playing, singing, and listening. The sound waves produced by music are a very powerful force and can stimulate us, relax us, excite us, and even alarm us. The type of music you chose to sing, play, or listen to should generate the mood you wish to create.

If you want to sing (see page 132) don't forget to chant, clap, dance, and shout as well. Listen to a recording, a live concert, a street musician, or even the haunting natural music of a wind chime (see page 74).

If you want to play a musical instrument and have no time to learn, play a drum (see page 97) or a penny whistle or strum a guitar. Plonk an old piano. You don't have to know the notes.

Bang, shout, clap and dance, whoop and let all the stress out.

Tinker with something mechanical

It's sometimes very relaxing to do something purely for the fun of it, for enjoyment, with no long-term goal. Breaking down mechanical things into bits serves no real purpose apart from relaxing us and giving us insight into how things work.

WHAT TO TAKE APART

Old clocks are one of the most enjoyable things to take apart—all those coils and springs are simply fascinating. Stereos and radios are fun as well. Avoid televisions or computer monitors as they may be dangerous. Old computers—safely unplugged—are fantastic fun to take apart and tinker with, containing all those wires and transistors and things that only an expert could name.

Find old mechanical things at your local landfill. Or try charity stores, rummage sales, and garage sales. You could even ask at the local watch and clock menders, as they sometimes chuck out things that are beyond repair. Ask relatives, neighbors, and friends—everyone has something they want to get rid of.

Meditate

Someone once said that if prayer is talking to God, then meditating is listening to the answer. And that's what you are going to do—listen. Meditating is very calming, superbly relaxing, and a very useful chill-out technique. No need to take on board any New Age ideas or change your diet—just listen. By listening you can learn a lot about what you are saying to yourself. By listening you can find a peace and tranquillity that is seldom reached in this busy world. By listening we shut up for a moment and allow our hearts to speak. By listening we shut off our mind and its constant cacophony of complaints and worries.

WHAT DO YOU HAVE TO DO?
Find somewhere to sit comfortably where you won't be disturbed. Let your hands fall naturally into your lap and close your eyes. Allow all tension in your neck and shoulders to drop away. Shrug your shoulders up to your ears and then let them drop.

Concentrate on your breathing. Breathe in through your nose

and out through your mouth. With each intake of breath mentally say the word "calm." With each breath out mentally say the word "relaxed." Let your breathing be very still, very relaxed, and very unlabored.

Breathe for about ten minutes like this, and then slowly return to normal and see how relaxed you feel. You can do this on the train, in the office, waiting for a bus, while watching television, or even in the bath. If anyone interrupts you and you don't want to say you were meditating, you can just say you were thinking deeply or daydreaming.

You can certainly try the technique while walking. Or you might like to try a Zen walking meditation.

ZEN WALKING MEDITATION

Go for a walk alone in the countryside or in a park, somewhere green and picturesque. This is a walk with no purpose apart from relaxing. You aren't walking your dog or going anywhere in particular. You aren't exercising or getting fit. You are going to go for a walk purely and simply to relax. Don't look around you, but focus ahead so you can see where you are going, but don't look at any object in particular.

Let thoughts come into your mind, but always try to remember that you are walking to meditate, not think. Feel the motion of your body through the countryside and be aware of the feel of the air on your face, the smells, and the sense of being outdoors.

Allow your breathing to be very relaxed and come from your stomach rather than your upper chest. Occasionally take a deep breath to free up any tension you may have. Allow about twenty minutes several times a week to walk purely for pleasure and relaxation with no other purpose.

As you walk count your steps until you reach one hundred and then start again. As you start counting again, empty your mind as if you are emptying the numbers out of it. If you don't count—or recite a mantra (a repeated word such as "om")—your mind will fill up the empty space with idle chatter.

Dress a tree with ribbons

Ribbon dressing for trees is an ancient pagan tradition. In the distant past, trees were decorated for fun, for ritual, for celebration, and for commemoration. Trees were venerated and worshiped, and the need to decorate them still exists in modern times— Christmas trees being the prime example.

Ribbon dressing is great fun and very therapeutic. It puts us in touch with our ancestors and restores us to our proper place in the natural world—the world of trees.

You can decorate a tree that already exists in your backyard, or you could buy one. Choose bright ribbons and tie them on wherever you feel they belong. A tree decorated with ribbons coming alive in the wind is a heart-warming sight.

You can add wind chimes for a musical accompaniment (see page 74). You don't have to restrict yourself to ribbons alone. You can use colored yarn, streamers, strips of kitchen foil, string, beads, glass balls, ornaments—or anything you might use to decorate your Christmas tree.

There's an old English tradition of decorating trees with unusual objects. A famous gardener has a teapot tree. He collects— and is given—teapots that he hangs on an old tree. There are now hundreds of teapots in this wacky tree, and it is quite a talking point. It reminds him of his childhood when his nanny used to do a similar thing to liven up a dull afternoon. What will you hang on your tree?

Go running

Running doesn't just keep you fit. It also increases your awareness, enhances your appreciation of life, boosts your metabolism, develops your responsiveness, and gets you out and about in the fresh air, looking around at your local environment and, of course, moving faster than usual. All these things come together to make you a happier and more relaxed person.

GET OUT THERE

Running addicts—and there are lots of them—will tell you that it is an enjoyable and immensely rewarding activity. You really do have to get out there and find out for yourself.

The treadmill in the gym is useful if you want to keep fit, but its boring, repetitive action is no substitute for a hearty run in the open air. This is running as a chill-out technique rather than simply as a fitness technique.

Get out into the park and choose a distance you would like to run. It doesn't have to be far, especially if you aren't the fittest person in the world. Try finding two trees or lamp posts to run between. Don't be too ambitious at this stage: you don't want to put yourself off! Aim for a distance of no more than two hundred yards to begin.

GETTING STARTED

Begin running slowly until you get into your stride. First, concentrate on the movement of your limbs as you build up your speed. Next, pay attention to the refreshing feeling of the air rushing against your face.

As you start to run faster, take a look at your surroundings. Notice how things appear to move differently when you approach them at a faster speed. Listen to the way the sounds around you change their pitch and timbre as you run past.

Last, monitor how your body feels as you cover more of your distance. As soon as you feel exhausted or out of breath, stop. Start again when you have recovered. Record how long each run takes you and see how your times improve over as little as a week.

Sketch

Relaxing is all the more enjoyable if we have something to do while we chill out. Sketching is a marvellous way to spend a little time, as it encourages us to look around us, be creative, and switch off our minds. Sketching is a form of meditation. While we are busy doodling something happens to us, and when we stop, we find ourselves in a more relaxed frame of mind entirely.

Before you rush out and buy expensive sketchpads and pencils, try raiding the kids' art box first. Ordinary paper and a pencil is all you need to begin with. You can always stock up on the pricey stuff later.

Start by sketching things that don't move. Arrange some flowers in a vase or fruit in a bowl. Try sketching your own portrait viewed in a mirror. Once you've done this, move onto more difficult subjects; how about trying to draw your kids or your pets?

This isn't about capturing reality. Sketching in this context is a slightly more advanced form of doodling, of emptying the contents of your mind onto your sketchpad. You don't have to show anyone your sketches. Just enjoy the feeling of relaxation it brings.

Make a patchwork quilt

A patchwork quilt speaks of log fires, snowy winters, mulled wine, laughing children all curled up together, stories by the fire, long walks, time to write poetry and make things, and being snug and warm—romantic images that generate feelings to match.

MAKING A SIMPLE QUILT

Use a plain, heavy blanket as a backing. Cut out as many pieces of fabric as catch your eye—offcuts of fabric, dishcloths, a design from an old sweatshirt, some patches of colored wool, or a pennant or flag. Use fabric from garments or items that have personal, sentimental value to make a quilt of memories. Start by pinning on all the pieces of fabric until you have a design you're happy with. Overlap any you want. Then sew them to the blanket and take out the pins as you go. If you are accomplished at sewing, use delicate stitches, but it doesn't really matter—you can use huge, messy stitches if you like. You'll end up with a heavy patchwork quilt that is unique, unusual, and very personal. Stay warm and enjoy the winter curled up in it as you tell stories by the fire.

Trace your family tree

Tracing your family tree is an absorbing and quietly contemplative chill-out technique. There is nothing better on a winter's evening than poring over dusty documents, ancient birth certificates, and old photographs. And with each new person you discover, you uncover a wealth of history, a life lived long ago full of hope and adventure. Imagine unlocking ancient family secrets. It's great for a sense of belonging to delve into your roots, your heritage, and your genetic background.

DRAWING YOUR TREE

Any family tree you intend to trace will always begin with yourself. So put your name at the top of a piece of paper. Now draw two lines underneath to represent your parents—write their names in. Beside your name add the names of your siblings. Now from each parent draw two lines for your four grandparents. If you draw a blank on any of these names, leave their name space blank. You'll probably be able to fill it in later as you uncover more information.

ASK THE FAMILY

Now the project starts to get interesting. Add eight lines for your eight great-grandparents to your family tree. Now you need to start asking questions. Ask your parents, your uncles and aunts, and your grandparents if they are alive. Fill in the blanks as you slowly find out who's who in your family history. Go as far back as your relatives can remember. It's fascinating to find out more and more details about your family's past. You may find an eccentric great-great grandmother who traveled the world, or an ancestor who fought in an important battle in a distant war.

DETECTIVE WORK

To go even further back in the history of your family, you need to cast your net wider and use your powers of detection. Look in old archives and libraries at birth certificates, census returns, and local maps. The Internet is a very useful tool for tracing your ancestors: simply do a search for your family name and see what it comes up with!

chill out

Make your own ice cream

If you really want to chill out, what could be better than eating your own homemade ice cream while you laze in the sunshine in your hammock (see page 82)? You don't need expensive equipment or fancy gadgets to make your own delicious ice cream. All you need is a fridge, a bit of time, and the capacity to have some fun. Serving your own ice cream at a dinner party speaks of care and love for your guests. Anyone can go out and buy some ice cream, but only a really thoughtful person makes their own. This attention will be rewarded.

You will need just a few ingredients and a couple of 1 1/2 pint plastic containers with lids or, if your freezer compartment isn't big enough, a couple of ice trays and some aluminum foil to cover them.

Set the freezer to its lowest setting. Separate the eggs and whisk the yolks in a small bowl until well blended. In a bigger bowl, whisk the egg whites until they form stiff peaks. Beat in the sifted confectioners' sugar a little at a time until you've used it all. Slowly whisk the blended egg yolks with the meringue mixture.

Lightly whip the cream until it's frothy and forms stiff peaks. Fold this into the egg mixture and add any flavoring you want—this could be a dash of raspberry juice or chocolate syrup, a handful of crushed blackberries or strawberries, some chunks of fudge or chocolate chips, or any other flavoring you fancy. Mix thoroughly, and pour the ice cream into your container or ice trays. Cover and freeze for at least two hours before serving, eating, and chilling out.

HOMEMADE ICE CREAM

4 ounces sifted confectioners' sugar
4 eggs
1/2 pint heavy cream
flavoring of your choice (see recipe)

HONEY ICE CREAM

This is a truly exquisite taste sensation. You need:

1 pound fresh picked raspberries

$\frac{1}{4}$ pint heavy cream

1 8-ounce carton plain yogurt

10 level tablespoons of runny honey

2 tablespoons of lemon juice

A pinch of salt

4 egg whites

Run the raspberries through a sieve and add the cream, yogurt, honey, lemon juice, and salt. Mix thoroughly, put into ice trays, and freeze for at least three hours, but preferably overnight. Pop out of the trays, put into a bowl and stir until smooth. Then fold in the stiffly whisked egg whites. Return mixture to ice trays and refreeze. Leave for two hours and serve in long thin chilled glasses. Perfect after a heavy meal.

Sing

Ever suffered from road rage? Ever felt totally stressed and tense driving a car? Ever wondered what to do about it? Easy. Try singing. Singing is a great release. It lifts us emotionally to another realm, one where we feel elated and naturally high. And no one will know that you're doing it!

You don't have to be able to sing in tune, know the words, or even sing anything recognizable. Being able to lift your voice in song is enough. Singing is making music with your voice and is a very ancient tradition indeed. Humans have sung as long as they have been able to talk. By singing we put ourselves in touch with our hearts and our instincts. Singing is the most natural gift in the world.

Buddhist chanting is a form of singing—make the "om" sound to create interesting vocal patterns. Or sing up and down scales.

But the best place to let off steam and sing your heart out is in the shower. There's something cathedral-like in the hollow echoes that enable us to practice opera, sing chorales, belt out pop and rock really loudly, sing anything we want—and take no notice of the banging on the door.

Make a scrapbook

We all need interests outside work and home. Keeping mentally active keeps us from becoming stale and dull.

Keeping a scrapbook is a way of monitoring your passions. Perhaps you're keen on sports—then keep a scrapbook of how your local team fares, their mementoes, their scorecards, their team colors, brochures, flags, and pennants. Chart their progress and keep a record of their history.

Keep several scrapbooks going at once—one for each of your interests. An old-fashioned gray page scrapbook will do—they are very evocative of childhood. Collect various items of interest and stick them in or fold them between the pages—even draw and write in it.

Once you have kept a scrapbook for a short time it quickly becomes clear how useful it is. It's an easily accessible record that soon builds into something substantial. Keep one of your own life. Chart your own progress. Fill the pages with photos of yourself as a child, as a teenager, then as an adult. Collect scraps of poems, drawings you've done, and pressed flowers that have meant something to you. A scrapbook can form a marvelous heirloom to pass down to your children's children.

chill out

Create some calligraphy

Calligraphy doesn't have to be ornate or overly elaborate, just well formed and pleasing. It is good use of a good pen. And that's what you need first—a good pen. You can't practice calligraphy with a ballpoint pen, a pencil, a highlighter, or a felt-tipped pen. You need a fountain pen, one of the old-fashioned sort.

CHOOSING YOUR PEN

There is nothing quite so satisfying as writing with a proper fountain pen. The way the ink flows is enchanting. The way the nib eases its way across the paper is hypnotic and magical. Choosing the right fountain pen for you is something that takes time and mustn't be hurried. A fountain pen is a very personal thing. You'll need to try out quite a few before you find the right one. Go to a store that specializes in good pens and ask to try some out. Take pleasure in experimenting, using the pens quickly and slowly, making bold flourishes, and signing your name. They can be quite expensive, but they last for many years so they're a good investment.

USING YOUR PEN

Once you've bought your fountain pen you can start practicing your calligraphy. Choose a color of ink that reflects your personality—green for creative types, purple for perfectionists, gray for musical people, brown for writers and artists, red for warm vital people, black for the serious, turquoise for spiritual people, light blue for those in touch with their feminine side, dark blue for those in touch with their masculine side and medium blue for very balanced people.

Once you've filled your pen, use a good quality paper—smooth but absorbent—to try out your flourishes and letters. Start with your signature first and write it again and again until you are happy with it. You can change it. There's no reason to stick with a signature that doesn't reflect the new you.

PRACTICING LETTERS

Calligraphy doesn't have to be about perfection. It's about good penmanship, which can mean what you want it to mean. Calligraphy is a personal thing.

When you are happy with the way you write, then that is your own personal calligraphy.

Of course, if you want to display your writing, it will need to be really good to impress others. Practice whenever you write anything. In the modern world of word processors and computers, none of us writes as much as we might once have done. We get out of the habit of writing in longhand. Take pride in writing out your shopping list or signing a check. Enjoy the process of forming letters into words, words into sentences, and sentences into whole pages. Calligraphy can be quite addictive and tremendously satisfying.

HOW CHILLED OUT IS CALLIGRAPHY?

Very chilled indeed. Once you are a superior penperson you become confident in all areas of your life. Those who have scrappy, untidy writing are often scrappy and untidy in their thinking. You, on the other hand, are supremely organized, relaxed, and confident.

Embroider a sampler

Making a sampler is very relaxing. It is something you can do while chatting or watching television. It occupies your hands and mind on a very tranquil level—almost like a meditation.

If you've never done embroidery before it doesn't matter. What matters is that you try new things, experiment, and have fun. You will need a piece of plain fabric, a frame, colored thread, and a needle.

Buy a frame from a craft store, or make one yourself out of a bamboo cane bent round into a circle. Loosely stitch your plain fabric to it so you have a tight circle to work on. Or make a square one out of an old picture frame.

Traditionally samplers have a basic design—perhaps a house, some flowers, or a row of people—and a full alphabet, your date of birth, and your name. Easy.

Lightly draw your design in pencil on the fabric so you have some guidelines to follow. Then stitch where you've penciled. Make the stitches any size you want, but the smaller the stitches you use, the neater it will look. Use any color thread you want. All knots and joins in the thread should be on the reverse so that the topside looks neat.

Once you've gotten the hang of it, be adventurous and add detail—if you have embroidered a house, add some windows and doors or a tree or two.

Make a pictogram of your life

Looking back over our lives—or even the recent past—we sometimes get a very distorted view. We remember only the failures and the downsides. If we put our lives into a pictogram, we get a more balanced overview. And balance is essential if we are to chill out and enjoy ourselves in a relaxed and happy way.

Creating a pictogram allows us to represent our lives in images in a very real and positive way. We feel better, inspired, and immensely cheered.

What visual images would you chose to represent your life? Perhaps a baby for when you first started off. Now all those Sunday color supplements you never read come into play. They're full of useful images to cut out. Start with a blank board as big as you can get it—four feet by two feet is ideal. Cut out the picture of the baby and stick it right in the middle. Now find some pictures of children playing and growing. Surround the baby with its childhood. If yours wasn't too happy then rewrite it—

choose happy pictures. You can overlap pictures or even cover some up entirely. They are still there, much as your past is still there, but buried under layers of what you have become.

Add pictures to represent you as a growing teenager and young adult—at school, at college, and working at your first job. Add pictures to represent your dreams, goals, aspirations, and ambitions—even the unfulfilled ones, they are still a part of you. Add pictures of your relationships—your spouse, your children, your work colleagues. Gradually build these pictures up around the original baby picture, just as you have been surrounded by love yourself.

Add pictures of friends, loved ones, vacations, travel, hobbies, and interests, and your pictogram will grow with you. Add pictures over the coming months as new things occur to you, and see your life as bright and interesting, vivid and colorful.

It's a wonderful way to look at life!

Grow an herb garden

Herbs don't take up much space. You could quite easily grow an herb garden on your kitchen windowsill. Ideally, herbs should be grown outdoors where the sun and rain can provide them with all the natural nutrition they need. But wherever you grow them, herbs can be used for many purposes—cooking, healing, ritual blessings and purification, and to help you improve and enrich your life physically, spiritually and emotionally. Nothing puts us more in touch with nature—and thus our true selves—than helping living things grow. We find such simplicity in nature that we cannot help but be more relaxed. There is something so reassuring in the cycle of the seasons, the slow steady progress of plants, and the enjoyment of eating what we have grown.

CHOOSING HERBS TO GROW

If you want herbs for cooking then choose the ones you use most—basil, chives, rosemary, sage, thyme—or if you want herbs to make refreshing teas (very relaxing) then try growing lemon balm, rosehips, peppermint, camomile, and valerian. Healing herbs include aniseed, bergamot, caraway, camomile, dill, elderflower, fennel, and lemon balm.

HOW TO GROW HERBS

Most herbs like a well-drained soil in a sunny place, protected from frost and wind. They do very well on a sunny windowsill as they are protected and nurtured there. If you plant them in your garden, dedicate a part of the garden just to herbs. Protect them from the ravages of insects and disease. Investigate companion planting—this is where you plant a beneficial plant nearby to protect against insects or disease. You may find that the herbs act as companion plants to your vegetable crops. Planting basil near tomatoes keeps them free of insects, and planting rosemary near carrots keeps them free of aphids and carrot fly. On the other hand you might want to attract certain insects.

Plant borage, bergamot, hyssop, and thyme near any beans, tomatoes, or squash plants as they all attract bees, which these plants need for pollination. Plant chervil, dill, and fennel to attract hoverflies, whose larvae eat aphids. And plant nasturtiums, whose flowers and seeds are useful in cooking, to keep the aphids off other plants.

DRYING HERBS

To dry sprigs of herbs for cooking it is important to collect them when they are quite dry—not after a rainfall, for instance. Hang them up in small, loose bunches head-down in a warm, dark place and leave for about a week. Only the strongest tasting herbs (such as bay leaves or lovage) are suitable for drying. But collect the seeds of herbs to use in cooking. Hang the seed heads upside down over a piece of white paper (so you can see the seeds when they drop). When they are ready they will fall by themselves. Store them in an airtight container until you want to use them.

Go on a mental journey

A guided meditation is exactly that—a meditation through which you are guided. Guided meditations can be bought as recordings but it is better to make up your own. They usually take you on a mental journey through specific locations designed to help you relax and become very chilled out. To give you an example of what they are like, you might like to record the following onto a cassette tape and play it back. Find somewhere comfortable where you won't be disturbed. Lie back and listen to the sound of your own voice taking you on an incredible journey into the very heart of your own relaxation.

GUIDED MEDITATION

Close your eyes and just listen. You are going on a journey. Imagine you are walking along a leafy country lane. It is warm and very pleasant. You feel relaxed and comfortable. As you walk, you enjoy the sensation of the sunlight playing through the dappled leaves on your bare face. You feel relaxed and happy. As you walk, you notice that the

path is gradually going downwards and is gently sloping. The trees begin to thin out, and you are leaving the leafy lane and beginning to walk along a little path. The ground beneath your feet is beginning to get sandy, and you notice you have bare feet. The sand feels good under your toes.

There are no trees now, and you have come out into the sunshine. On either side of you there are sand dunes covered in grasses. As you walk, you hear the sounds of the sea in the near distance and sea gulls are wheeling overhead. You feel relaxed and happy.

You continue down the path until you reach the beach. The sea is lazy and blue, and there is no one on the beach except you.

You walk along the edge of the sea, and the water on your feet feels cool and invigorating. The beach stretches away into the distance, and the sun is warm on your face. You feel relaxed and at peace with the world.

In the distance you make out a figure walking towards you. You recognize the

figure. It is the person you love most in all the world. You begin to run towards the person, and the person runs towards you. As you draw nearer, both running, you hold out your arms to each other. You throw yourselves into each other's arms and hug like you've never been hugged before. This is where you are supposed to be, this is like coming home. You look up into the person's face and see it is yourself. The two of you merge to become one, and you are relaxed and totally calm and peaceful. You open your eyes and find you are back in your own room still feeling calm, relaxed, and at peace with the world.

Obviously this is an example. Now you can begin to make changes to make the guided meditation suit you. Enjoy, have fun, relax, and chill out.

Make a dream catcher

Dream catchers, legendary objects made by Native Americans to catch and rid themselves of unwanted dreams, can be made in many shapes and sizes. They are not only useful but also bright and colorful and make interesting decorations in your bedroom. In the center of a dream catcher you will see a colored bead known as iktome, the spider—the keeper of dreams.

You need a freshly cut bamboo stem about two feet long or a fresh hazel twig or something equally flexible. You also need some twine—fishing line or strong cotton both work well—some feathers, a bead or two, and some ribbons.

Curl the bamboo or hazel into a circle and fasten it by wrapping twine around it. Cut off any sharp ends and conceal the join by wrapping one of the ribbons around it, to form a basic circle. You may cover all of the bamboo or hazel in ribbon or just a small section.

Tie one end of the twine onto any point on the circle and thread it across about a quarter of the circle. Tie it and cut if off. Come back a bit towards your starting point and tie another cross twine across the circle. Do this four times until you have four lengths around the circle.

From the center of each of these tie one twine to each of the other three. This gives a sort of cat's cradle effect. Experiment until you have a pleasing criss-cross of lines looking like a spider's web. Don't forget to add a bead in the center to represent the spider.

Tie some ribbons from the bottom of the circle, and add some feathers and beads to these downward hanging ribbons.

HOW TO USE YOUR DREAM CATCHER

When you wake each morning, take your dream catcher to your bedroom window and "empty" it—tap it on the windowsill to tip out the bad dreams. My small son suffered nightmares until I made him one of these. He hasn't had a single bad dream since—and still empties his dream catcher every morning without fail, just in case.

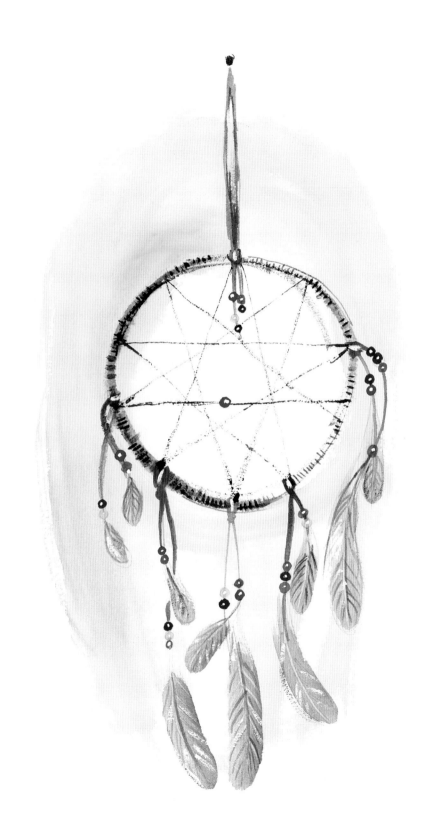

Memorize a poem

If you can memorize poetry, you will always have a helping hand with you when you are in need. Some of the best inspirational words that have ever been written are in the form of poetry—words to inspire us, calm us, give us confidence, and motivate us.

Start with very short poems (see page 111) that you can commit to memory easily and quickly. Don't try to learn the whole thing by heart straightaway—start with a line a day and let that line be an inspiration to you that day. The next day learn the next line.

Choose poets who write in our everyday language, that way you can memorize them much more easily. Save the Shakespeare and Chaucer for when you are really good at this. Try this one for starters:

Flower in the crannied wall,
I pluck you out of the crannies,
I hold you here, root and all, in my hand,
Little flower—but if I could understand
What you are, root and all, and all in all,
I should know what God and man is.

This evocative poem was written in the mid-nineteenth century by Alfred, Lord Tennyson.

Once you've mastered one poem, you can go on to build up the poetry collection in your head bit by bit.

Keep a nature box

Keeping a nature box takes us back to our childhood, when the long summer days stretched away forever, and we had nothing better to do than watch an ant making its way across the lawn or the erratic flight of a butterfly. These were the best days of our lives, indeed.

First, find a box. Any attractive wooden box will do— cigar boxes are perfect for the job. Those old printer's trays that seem to inhabit yard sales are ideal since they have lots of little compartments. If you want a really special box, ask a local carpenter to make one up for you.

WHAT SHALL I PUT IN?

Keeping a nature box broadens your horizons and keeps you looking out for interesting bits of nature—dragonfly cases, discarded butterfly pupae, a smal fossil, an acorn or two, a bird's nest after the bird has finished using it, a dead hornet, wool, feathers, shells, fir cones, crab claws, crystals, moss, owl pellets, seaweed, seashells, sticky buds, twigs, lichen, cuttlefish, or a snakeskin. These are just a few items in my own nature box collected over a very short period while out walking in the countryside or on the seashore.

Be positive!

As small children we are told "don't," "mustn't," "stop," and "no." Rarely are we told "yes," "go on," "do it," "you can." We learn to hold back, live in fear, and we are reluctant to take risks or challenge ourselves. You can change your life by making positive affirmations.

HOW THEY WORK

Affirmations work on a very deep level, far too deep for us to consciously understand. As long as we follow a few basic guidelines, they are very effective in making us more daring and more adventurous in our lives. They also help restore the balance between emotion and reason. What we dare hope for becomes a reality.

GUIDELINES

Never leave room for doubt. If you want to be more confident say to yourself "I am confident." That's plain and simple—no room for misunderstanding or indecision. If you say, "I will be confident"—when will you be more confident? And if you say, "I am getting more confident," it leaves room for your subconscious to question. More confident than what? More confident than you were yesterday or five years ago? Use affirmations that leave no room for doubt. Say "I am" rather than "I will be" or "I am getting."

WHEN TO USE THEM

Affirmations work best if they are used repeatedly. Write them down on sticky notes and post them in prominent places around your home— on the mirror, on the refrigerator, on the telephone. Then you'll see them all the time in your everyday life. Every morning, as soon as you wake and your

conscious brain hasn't had a chance to kick in, say them out loud 30 or 40 times. Last thing at night, just as your head hits the pillow, say them again out loud—make sure you fall asleep while saying them.

Over just a short period of time you will notice quite a difference. If you are using the "I am confident" affirmation, you will find yourself bolder and more outgoing. If you are using an affirmation for relaxation, such as "I am calm," you will notice within days a more relaxed outlook on life, a steadying of the nerves, and a more optimistic approach to everything you do.

WHAT NOT TO USE

Affirmations work best if they are left to work on you. They don't work on the outside world around you. You can say "I am happy," and you will notice a difference quite quickly. But try saying "I am rich," and you won't see much change at all. That's because affirmations work on a deep level within you —not on your bank manager. They also work best if left to work on the emotional side of you rather than the physical. Saying "I am slim" might work over a long period of time, but it might be more effective and productive to keep saying "I eat less" or "I exercise more."

Affirmations work only if you do them, say them, read them, and live them. A life without affirmations is a little like owning a car but keeping it in the garage—you ain't going anywhere. But jump in and start the engine, and you can start to go places. It's easy—start your new life now!

Learn to knit

Just because your granny did it doesn't mean it won't benefit you. Grannies know a thing or two about relaxing, which is often why they have lived so long! Knitting is very absorbing, therapeutic and, of course, useful. There is a real satisfaction in choosing pretty colors of yarn and creating your own fabric. And if your first attempt at knitting results in nothing more useful than a misshapen, hole-ridden woolen strip, you will have concentrated, relaxed for a while, turned off your television or your computer, learned a new skill, and amused yourself in a very simple and time-honored way.

LEARNING TO KNIT

Knitting is far easier to try than to read about. Even a textbook with diagrams makes it look a lot more complicated than it actually is. Go and find someone to show you how it's done—perhaps your mother or grandmother. Once you have been shown how to hold the needles and the yarn plus a few basic stitches, it's easy to get going!

YOUR FIRST PROJECT

Start with something very simple. A scarf, being simply a long, knitted strip, is the easiest garment to start with. That way you have no difficult sleeves or necklines to do. Gather together lots of balls of brightly colored chunky yarn—ask all the knitters among your friends and family for leftovers—and invest in a big pair of knitting needles. Cast on 40 stitches, and keep knitting! There is no need to stop at a particular place. Just carry on knitting until it looks long enough for you! A scarf is useful for the winter, too—it's strange, but there seems to be nothing warmer than a scarf you knitted yourself.

MOVING ON

Mastering knitting is easy, and you can build your skills very quickly. Once you've finished your scarf—and this can take a while if you chose to make it an especially long one—you can move onto more difficult items. For this you'll need to learn the ins and outs of fancy stitches and shaping. Happy knitting!

Read for fun

We all read company reports, technical documents, and newspapers to find out what is going on in the world; textbooks to improve our education; magazines to provide quick entertainment fixes; plus Internet pages, bank statements, and bills. But when did you last read a book entirely for fun?

BLOCKBUSTERS

We may buy a blockbusting novel at the airport. But we shouldn't keep this pleasure just for vacation time. Make time in your day to read. Reading for fun is relaxing and entirely indulgent—what could be better for chilling out?

WHAT'S BATMAN UP TO?

Reading for fun doesn't just have to mean books. Go back to your childhood and read comics—when did you last dip in and see what Batman's up to these days? And how about reading out loud? It's marvellously therapeutic, even if you only read out loud to yourself. There is something about the sound of your voice that is very soothing. And don't forget children's books. Many adults rediscovered reading for fun with the Harry Potter books—just make sure you don't get caught stealing the latest volume from your kids.

Design a maze

Mazes are amazing. They are a ritual way of walking a set path to clarify our thoughts, focus our attention, and crystallize our goals. They can be walked for mediation, for spiritual contemplation, or for just getting lost in to remind ourselves of where we need to be. Mazes as a fun entertainment are still popular, but they are equally powerful as a visual and ritualistic aid to meditation. The getting lost business was originally part of an initiate's induction into deeper and secret mysteries.

DESIGNING YOUR MAZE

Map out the design of your maze on paper first. A good maze should start at the outside and continue through a pre-ordered series of twists and turns until it reaches the center. Make sure your design is regular and ordered. There don't have to be any blind alleys or dead ends. It might be a just a simple, circular pattern that gradually spirals to the center, or a series of left and right turns drawn out on a square grid. You could also use a series of paths within a square or a triangle where all the turns are at 60 degrees to each other. A very spiritual maze can be made using a figure eight and keeping your path overlapping until it reaches the center. The native peoples of Peru used complex bird and animal shapes to outline their mazes.

Designing a maze and drawing a mandala for meditation (see page 92) are very similar—you might like to think

Your maze can be completely visible. Create one on a lawn or grassy area using pebbles or twigs. If you want a more permanent arrangement you can use standing stones, hedges, walls, wood, railings, fencing, or a plant-covered trellis. If you have enough space, you could even plant trees to map out your maze.

While you are on vacation, it can be a beautifully spiritual thing to do to lay out pebbles on a beach in a simple spiral. Walk your maze at dawn, in a meditative state of mind, before the tide comes in and covers your work.

of your mandala as a picture of your maze. They both serve the same purpose—to draw you into the very center of your being. The smaller, one-dimensional mandala does it by focusing your thoughts and the larger, three-dimensional maze by focusing your body.

BUILDING YOUR MAZE

You don't need to get lost in a maze, and you don't need high walls or hedges.

RITUAL WALKING

Mazes were often used to clear people's thinking. You entered the maze with a problem and focused on the center—by the time you arrived there, walking very slowly, you also arrived at the solution to your situation. The walking should always be done very slowly, in measured tread, with your attention firmly on the center—a sort of fixed trance to focus on a single goal.

Build a barbecue

Cooking and eating out-of-doors is a primitive need. Food tastes so much better outdoors. There is nothing better on a warm evening than to smell food cooking over an open fire with lots of tangy wood smoke. It satisfies an essential part of our emotional well-being.

THE SIMPLE MODEL

Barbecues can be as simple as a few rocks with a metal cooking grill resting on them. You can then light a fire between the rocks and cook over it when the flames have died down. You don't even need to use charcoal.

THE DELUXE MODEL

If you really want to go to town, build a barbecue out of brick. You need brick pillars on three sides with a flat top to rest the grill on. Even if your bricklaying skills are minimal and the finished barbecue looks a bit uneven—it doesn't matter. You have returned home to your hunter-gatherer existence and will get an immense feeling of contentment and satisfaction.

Once you've built your barbecue, don't limit yourself to cooking burgers or sausages. Try flame-roasted corn-on-the-cob, kebabs with lots of lovely slices of vegetables, whole cloves of garlic, stuffed grape leaves, chilies, spring rolls, or rice cakes. Take your wok outside and cook wonderful Chinese meals over a real fire.

Make a sculpture

Children like nothing better than to have their hands in clay, molding weird and wonderful shapes. These things are terribly satisfying and essential to human development. As we grow older, we lose touch with this need to shape and form. When we're stressed, taking a lump of clay and molding it can be enormously beneficial. As we squeeze and thump the clay, we lose our aggression and forget our worries.

DIFFERENT MATERIALS

Sculpture isn't just about clay. You can also use metal, wood, glass, paper, plant material (stems, twigs, grasses, flowers, sticks), fabric, concrete, plaster, and plastic. And there are many different ways of holding it all together—wire, mesh, a wooden framework, string, a cardboard box, sticks or twigs, stiff card, a glass bottle, or even a wastepaper basket. Look around for materials and use your imagination.

Have a rough idea of the sort of thing you want to make and let your intuitive and creative powers lead. That way you'll be happy with whatever you end up with, as your sculpture will become a symbolic representation rather than a recognizable likeness. Here's just one idea to get you started:

SCULPT A HUMAN HEAD

Start with some chicken wire with a fine mesh. Cut out a rectangle three feet by eighteen inches. Bend this around into a cylinder. Put on some thick gloves for safety, and then start to mold and shape the chicken wire into a ball. This will serve as your basic head shape Add another rectangular cylinder to make a neck for it to stand on. Mix up some plaster of Paris until you have a thick mixture. Using gloves again, smear this over the wire, but don't worry about covering it all—it looks most effective with some of the wire showing. Build this plaster up into a nose, eyebrows, eye sockets, and mouth. It doesn't have to look like anyone in particular—it doesn't even have to look lifelike. It's just an excuse to play and get in touch with the creative child within.

Make a ritual mask

The more cut off we are from our native origins the more stressed we become. Modern life offers nothing for our basic need to be tribal, to be primordial, to be primitive. Sometimes we need to cast off the shackles of our civilized selves and become once again an instinctive animal of the woods and forests. By making a ritual mask, we can reclaim our ancestral shape and form—and dance once more to the rhythm of the universe.

WHAT RITUAL MASKS REPRESENT

Native peoples know that when they adopt the mask of a certain animal they can take onboard that animal's spirit, and become part of that animal. Shamen can take it further; they can become a shape-shifter—and become the animal itself.

The ritual mask can represent an animal or a bird, a journey or an experience, a plant, or even an insect. Your ritual mask can represent any attribute of the natural world you wish to explore, to become, to experience. By journeying in another form you can feel and sense what other beings learn and know about the world.

YOUR MASK

Make a mask that contains the essence of the form without being an exact like-ness. If, for ritual purposes, you want to experience the stag, you don't need to make a full size mask complete with eye sockets, horns, face hair, ears, and a black, velvety nose. All you need is a pair of horns to represent the essential stag-ness of the beast. These can be tied on easily to a leather cap with eye slits. You become the stag without having to be the stag in form.

If you want to experience the thrill of the eagle, a few feathers attached to a simple eye mask would do. And if you want to become the green man of the woods, then a simple green face mask decorated with leaves, twigs, and acorns will suffice.

Perhaps you want to ritualize some quality of natural life or expression of living. Perhaps you would like to represent the wind itself. How would you show this on a mask? You might draw the dark lines of the wind on a white mask, or attach silver streamers or ribbons to represent the wind.

It might be the journey of the soul into the afterlife you want to ritualize. Make a mask that contains some essence of your life here, perhaps an enlarged photo of yourself with eye-holes cut in it in the right places. Overlaid on this you could attach whatever represents to you the soul's journey —two coins to pay the ferryman, white streamers to represent the white light, a crucifix to represent the Christian heaven, a black and white pebble for the Buddhists—whatever is your own personal representation.

Once you have made your mask, you can wear it to act out your own ritualized dance of whatever you have chosen to experience. This is best done in the woods or wild parts of the countryside, by a fire, and at dawn or dusk. See what happens. Expand your consciousness. Enjoy. Chill out.

chill out

Be your own guru

The day before the Buddha became the Buddha he was plain old Siddhartha Guatama. So what happened? What made the difference? Simple. He chose to become the Buddha. He made the decision to become his own guru, his own perfect master, his own enlightened teacher. This may be a little ambitious, but we can incorporate some of the Buddha's teachings into our own life. You don't have to become a Buddhist, just work with the principles of being your own guru.

WHAT IS A GURU?

A guru is someone who takes us from gu (darkness) to ru (light). They are wise teachers. We too, at times in our lives, have been wise teachers. Friends come to us for advice and help. Our children look to us for authority and guidance. Our parents increasingly hand over responsibility to us. Our employers give us duties that stretch us and make us wise. We are growing all the time.

HOW TO PLAY THE GURU GAME

Imagine someone comes to you with a question about the universe,

156

how it works, how it is put together. Imagine you are that wise teacher. Answer with whatever comes into your head. Your intuitive powers are greater than you think. The answer will fit.

Now imagine it is you that comes to you with such a question. You give yourself the answer. Begin by asking yourself "Oh, Great Wise One, what is the answer to..." Don't stop to think about the answer—just let your intuition guide you, and the answer will be there.

This is a fun game but it often sparks considerable insights into the nature of the universe. When we know, we understand. And when we understand, we are at peace.

MORE THAN A GAME

It might take practice—try it out with a good friend to give you confidence and get you going—but once you've perfected this technique it often goes quite beyond a game. You do indeed become your own guru and in turn become a happier, more well-rounded, and infinitely wiser person.

BUCKETS OF WATER

After all there are no secrets. Knowledge is like a gigantic pool of water. We all have a bucket and can all skim off some of the water of knowledge. The only difference between us and the Buddha is how deep we are prepared to sink our bucket, how much water we are prepared to haul in. Most people skim off the top inch or two of brackish water and think themselves clever. The guru is someone who lets the bucket sink to the bottom where the water is deep and clean and pure before pulling it in. That is why a guru is wise.

WHERE IS THE POOL?

The pool of water resides within you. There are no secrets. You can haul in as much of the water of knowledge as you choose. You can have the answers to any questions you choose to put to yourself. And the answers will be real. They are your answers to your questions. There is no one on earth who can say they are wrong.

You are your own guru.

chill out

Index

chill out